The Breast Book

The Breast Book

Attitude, Perception, Envy & Etiquette

Maura Spiegel & Lithe Sebesta

WORKMAN PUBLISHING · NEW YORK

Library of Congress Cataloging-in-Publication Data
Spiegel, Maura.
The breast book : attitude, perception, envy and etiquette / by Maura Spiegel and Lithe Sebesta.
p. cm
ISBN 0-7611-2112-9 (pbk. : alk. paper)
1. Breast—Social aspects. 2. Breast—Psychological aspects. 3. Breast—History.
I. Spiegel, Maura.   II. Title

GT498.B74 S42 2002
391.6—dc21

2001026985

Workman books are available at special discounts when purchased in bulk for premiums and sales promotions as well as for fund-raising or educational use. Special editions or book excerpts can also be created to specification. For details, contact the Special Sales Director at the address below.

Workman Publishing Company, Inc.
708 Broadway · New York, NY 10003-9555
www.workman.com

Printed in Hong Kong
First printing March 2002
10 9 8 7 6 5 4 3 2 1

ACKNOWLEDGMENTS

For insights, suggestions, a timely laugh, encouragement and friendship, we'd like to thank: Alison Akant, Amy Arbus, Jonathan Butler, Mary Campbell, Amy Carberg, Harold Cook, David Damrosch, Kira von Eichel, Florence Falk, Kenji Fujita, Shelley Geiler, Rochelle Gerstein, Elyse Goldstein, Michelle Gucovsky, Gina Heiserman, Regan Heiserman, Deanna Heindel, Vivien Heller, David Jacobson, Bronwyn Keenan, Ilsa Klinghoffer, Lisa Klinghoffer, Kip Kotzen, Nicole Krauss, David Lapoujade, Anna Levine, James Linville, George McClancey, Frank Meo, Kiki Miller, Adrienne Munich, Jack Murnhigan, Daniel Myerson, Silvana Paternostro, Lisa Perkins, Dan Polin, Natasha Randall, Virginia Reath, Andy Reichsman, Roo Rogers, Courtney Saunders, Alex Shear, Elizabeth Sheinkman, Alexandra Shiva, Tom Shone, Carole Slade, John Smyth, Ted and Virginia Solotaroff, Michelle Urry, Max Weiss and Deborah White.

And special thanks to Rosie Schaap and Cecily Dixon.

At Workman: Thanks to Ruth Sullivan, for her vision and her ability to refuse our excesses; to Lynn Strong, for being strict on the page and nice in person; and to Patty Bozza, Alexandra Truitt, Jerry Marshall, Jessica Firger, Janet Vicario, Leora Kahn, Margaret Lanzoni, Janet Parker and Janice Ackerman.

Thanks also to the historians whose fine research we drew from, especially Marilyn Yalom.

And boundless gratitude to our beloved and patient families: Leonard and Dawn Sebesta and Anne Mourek Sebesta; Charlotte Spiegel; Jill Spiegel; Arthur, Sam and Kate Heiserman.

CONTENTS

PREFACE: NAKED APES

Kept from us by glass, hairy, bent and frozen with puzzled expressions in faux-natural settings—the earth as we imagine it then—our evolutionary ancestors often seem more animal than human, more mammal than Homo sapiens. But human they are: not only because of their opposable thumbs and alleged cognitive abilities, but because of their swollen chests. Though, in the eighteenth century, the Swedish taxonomist Linnaeus named an entire class Mammalia, literally "of the breast"—choosing the breast, among a variety of common features, to denote what humans had in common with other species—humans are the only mammals

whose females have breasts that are permanently enlarged. While in other mammalian species the paps grow full only during lactation when the mother is suckling her young, female humans are perpetually endowed.

Evolutionists have pondered why women developed this outstanding trait. What adaptive function could permanent breasts have served in the evolution of the species? Darwinists have offered a host of theories, some attributing the evolution of these permanent orbs to their childrearing function, others to their role as sexual attractors. It could be that breasts evolved as signals to the male of female maturation, the soft orbs announcing when a female is reaching reproductive age. As a bonus, large breasts suggest good fat-retaining cells that promise good nursing capacity. One problem with this theory: breast size does not correlate to ability to nurse an infant efficiently.

MAMMAE

The Latin term for breasts, *mammae*, derives from the plaintive cry "mama," spontaneously given by the young from widely divergent linguistic groups.

Those more interested in breasts' erotic power speculate that in the period when our progenitors began to walk upright (in order for males to carry and throw spears while running), the female's frontal orbs evolved as mimic-buttocks. Since the front of the female lacked the rounded curves males associated with sexual arousal (presumably our ancestors had a taste for

Breasts are less prominent than belly and hips in this sixteenth-century painting by Leonardo da Vinci of Leda and the swan.

the doggie-style sexual approach), they evolved permanent breasts as a stand-in for buns! According to writer Desmond Morris, "If the female of our species was going to successfully shift the interest of the male round to the front, evolution would have to do something to make the frontal region more stimulating." (Morris contends that naked apes also sprouted earlobes, fleshy nostrils and everted lips in order for mates to arouse one another in repeat encoun-ters and once the

A manatee nurses calves underwater in a maternal, almost human, attitude.

thrill of a new conquest had faded—to make sex sexier as a way of advancing the practice of monogamy.)

Feminists naturally tell a different story. Enlarged breasts did not evolve to attract the male; they simply functioned as fat storage areas for females who evolved under nutritional stress. Ancestral humans walked long and far in search of food, and they needed fat storage for years of lactation. The fat layer, they argue, also cushioned the more fragile subtissue and helped to keep the milk warm, making the breast less a sexual signal to the male than a mechanism for improving the female's chance of keeping a child alive and healthy.

Still others say that breasts evolved so that mothers could feed their babies more comfortably. To have a baby nestling in the crook of the arm or resting on the lap, the nipple needed to be brought down low, and the baby required something pliant and convenient for its small hands to grab hold of. (In apes the baby grips the mother's fur and so needn't be supported by the mother's arms, but we're a hairless lot.) Less maternally oriented feminists have contended that the fatty tissue of the breast is simply a lure to attract men to fondle and caress the erogenous nipple, assuring women maximum sexual stimulation.

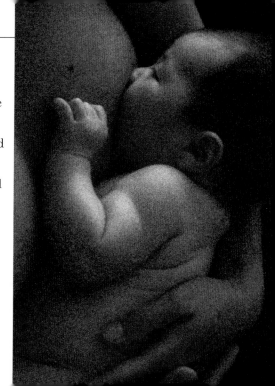

Since there are no breast fossils, it's hard to know when in human evolution breasts became permanently swollen. Science writer Natalie Angier contends that the permanently swollen breast is "nonfunctional to the point of being counterfunctional," and that its permanent swelling serves no evolutionary purpose whatsoever. For Angier, breasts are ornamental but not necessarily linked to erotic purposes; their attraction is purely aesthetic. Breasts are flamboyant and irresistible, but they are, evolutionarily speaking, "arbitrary." Perhaps their enticement, she suggests, is linked to a neural pathway that serves some other, unknown purpose, or

perhaps it is connected to the eye's tendency to be attracted to round objects and circles, like fruits and nuts, a mother's face or the moon.

INTRODUCTION

Breasts
"There is something between us."
—Donald Hall

Figurehead on sailing ship, c. 1800

oobs, bazoombas, tits, ta-tas, knockers; between us, around us or (in our case) attached to our chests: breasts are simply everywhere. Ours is a pneumatic universe, where breasts are not only constantly visible but under observation: noted, assessed, appreciated and deprecated; skylined or buried. Popping in and out of our peripheral vision and sight lines and between our subconscious and conscious worlds—breasts are front and center in almost every culture: from precivilized goddess figures to the digital (and bulletproof) frontals on today's Lara Croft.

But our breast obsession isn't and hasn't been universally shared. Traditional geishas in Japan, for example, wrap and de-emphasize their breasts for an austere (and erotic) self-presentation. In Middle Eastern cultures, the waist and hips are considered more appealing, and even in the Western sexual iconography breasts have faced competition for top billing: the buttocks and belly were at various points in history considered the most stimulating corporeal zones. Indeed, for many centuries in European culture, small breasts were more desirable than large ones.

And even today, the meaning of breasts' popularity is flattened into a one-syllable word: sex, as in SEXXX. It's not surprising that what you get when you type *breast* into an Internet search engine is 99 percent pornography

This book is an answer to breasts being fettered to sex in the cultural imagination, for the reality of breasts' impact is far less limited. In fact, the world according to breasts is almost overwhelmingly varied, inconceivably rich and far from wedded solely to heterosexual male fantasy. In cultural history, breasts have figured as symbols of liberation, or as machines of production; in art history, images of breasts have suggested ideas about maternity, eros and love; in commerce and medicine, breasts are big business; and so on. Breasts have a starring role in our psychic life, top billing in the drama of relations from womb to tomb—and they literally define what it means to be mammal. And don't

forget the very real presence of breasts every day: bouncing down the street, passing us on escalators or (in domestic bliss) being cupped in the palm.

When we first started research on this book project two years ago, we wondered if we would have enough information to fill 500 pages about breasts; we have ended by zealously cutting (a kind of nonsurgical breast reduction) and selecting the best from an expanding mammalian universe. For a portion of our research, we hit fashion archives, medical libraries, antique-book fairs and a collectibles and ephemera expert—who said, with a straight face, "Have you spoken to the

breast memorabilia person yet?" We felt sometimes there was no vacation from work; wherever we went, whether to galleries, museums, lingerie shops, saunas, Paris or our local deli, we were stalked by breasts and breast-related objects. Things shape-shifted around us: lamps and melons began to look suspiciously curved. In Las Vegas, we were offered a beer can with a reusable nipple top, and later, in the hotel lobby, pasties twinkled like disco balls. Ordinary excursions were transformed; changing at the gym became an exercise in not staring, and we finally—years too late—began to understand why teenage boys have only one thing on the brain.

Needless to say, there has been a certain comedy in looking at the world through these twin lenses. The puns, of course, became unavoidable. So we embraced them; it is, after all, a titillating topic. For if we now saw the world through breasts, the world now saw us in the same light: at our publisher's, we're known (politely) as "the Breast Ladies." We became temporary celebrities at cocktail parties—"Tell us a . . . titbit" was a typical opener—sparking up otherwise ordinary conversation with fascinating factlets and perhaps getting the kind of attention usually reserved for a large pair of knockers. (We were offered the research services of every man we met—and we politely declined.) We are now able to spot the word *breast* on a page at ten feet. What's between *us* is two years of thinking about breasts together; we've been joined, so to speak, bosom to bosom, *tit-à-tit.*

We have in fact had a very good time: if we began as friends, we're now bosom buddies. (Not to mention finding out that our breasts are neither as strange nor unique as we thought they were.) To be able to be playful and celebratory about breasts is a new, even uplifting, luxury. As beneficiaries of three decades of feminism, we now have what is in many ways the pleasure of looking at our breasts without breastplates—without the defensiveness against misogyny and misunderstanding. That isn't to say that we're not still vulnerable, or that our bodies are not as much a site of gender politics as they have always been, but simply that there is a greater latitude for lightheartedness without betrayal, irony without self-deprecation. Tit jokes are funny, now that we can make them, too—and now that the joke is no longer on us. This new freedom to admire breasts—sexually or otherwise—allows us to enjoy their versatility and their allure: the beautiful harmony of form and function that makes the breast a force of nature.

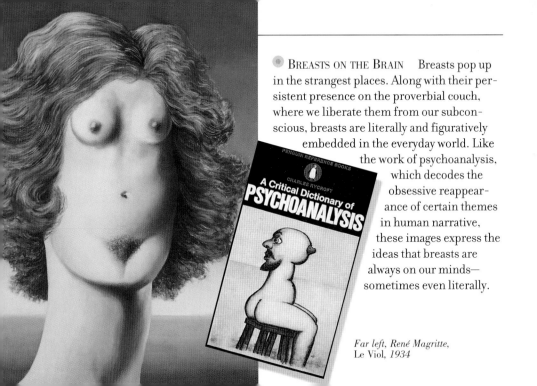

BREASTS ON THE BRAIN   Breasts pop up in the strangest places. Along with their persistent presence on the proverbial couch, where we liberate them from our subconscious, breasts are literally and figuratively embedded in the everyday world. Like the work of psychoanalysis, which decodes the obsessive reappearance of certain themes in human narrative, these images express the ideas that breasts are always on our minds— sometimes even literally.

Far left, René Magritte,
Le Viol, 1934

The Breast Book

An Embarrassment of Riches

"I will praise thee for I am fearfully and wonderfully made."
—*Psalm 139*

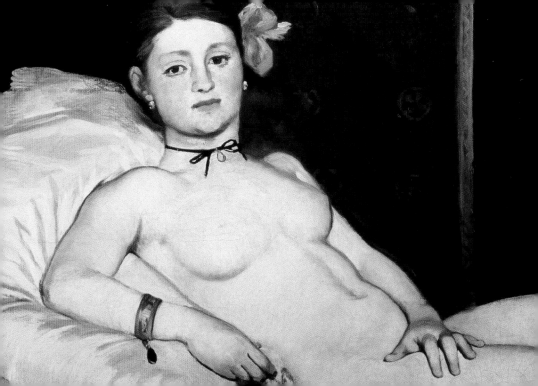

Real-life breasts, those that greet the day without benefit of makeup, airbrush or camera angling, really do demonstrate the wondrous variety of creation. Who could possibly imagine so *many* variations on a single theme? To be sure, breasts under sweaters look somewhat the same, give or take a few inches; only in the flesh do they let us know how singular they truly are. Each fresh pair brings a feeling of déjà vu, but then there's that small difference that makes the familiar strange; they're weightier than we thought, they sit higher or lower, the nipple is pinker or darker.

Previous page, Édouard Manet, Olympia; right, Jayne Mansfield with mini-me's

LOUDER THAN WORDS

Breasts, like noses, often convey a kind of personality: they can be boisterous or soft-spoken, generous or circumspect; they can be down-at-the-heel or upstanding citizens. As much as they belong to us, they also have a life all their own, and it's a bonus if their personality coincides with that of their owner. Sometimes a full-frontal dispute occurs: What's a demure woman to do with the chest of a good-time girl? Who wins the argument is a question of presentation. (What did you think those minimizers were for?)

"Why can't they just be normal?" is a common lament—but what's normal anyway within this remarkable spectrum? As with any of our features, to accept their quirks and eccentricities is generally a matter of time, and self-acceptance. For whatever their distinctive traits, breasts, like people, will find someone to love them.

Botero, Love Letters, *1968*

● "WHO'S THERE?"
Her alarmed posture
says modesty, but this
water nymph's breasts
are following a script of
their own. Their "come
hither" stance invites
approach—perhaps for
a cool drink of water.

"Tits. I understand tits. I have been studying tits since I was thirteen years old. I don't think there's any other organ or body part that evidences so much variation in size . . ."

"I know," replied Madeline, openly enjoying herself suddenly and beginning to laugh.
". . . There are women with breasts ten times the size of mine. Or even more . . . But are there people with noses ten times the size of mine? Four or five, max. I don't know why God did this to women."

—*Philip Roth*, Sabbath's Theater

Right, Joyce Tenneson, Nadya

*"On real women, I've seen breasts
that are as varied as faces: breasts
shaped like tubes, breasts shaped like
tears, breasts that flop down, breasts
that point up, breasts that are dominated by thick, dark nipples and
areolae, breasts with nipples so small
and pale they look airbrushed."*
—Natalie Angier

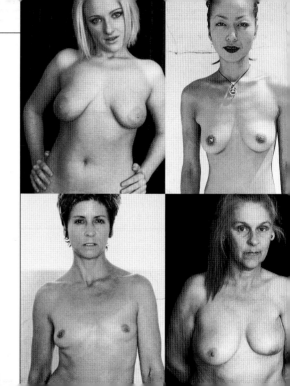

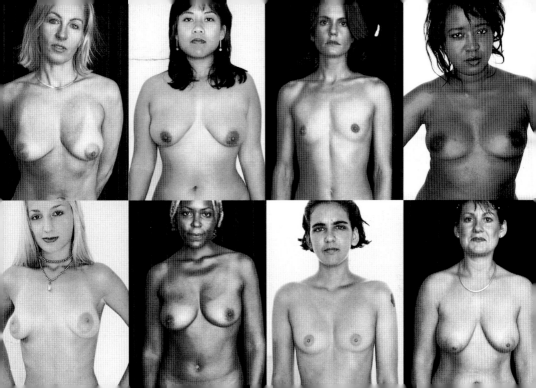

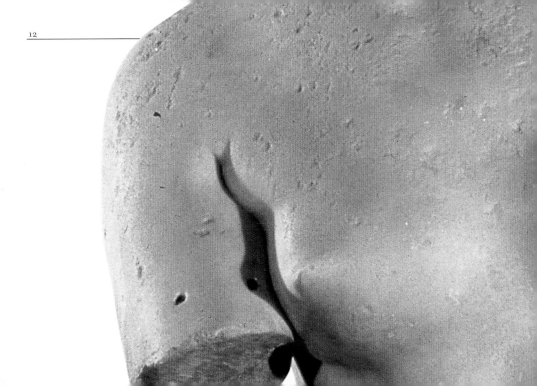

STONY LOOKS Modeled on improbability, marble statuary doesn't offer the feel of flesh—nor does it tussle with gravity. Set high and apart, these chiseled breasts represent impossible lovelinesses and seem at odds with the more realistic fleshiness of the thighs.

Left, Venus de Milo;
right, Venere di Cirene

MIXED AND MATCHED
Many women's breasts are unevenly matched, with one slightly larger—though evenness is often named as a feature of beauty. On the other hand, cold symmetry isn't always right either—there's something *off* in mirrored perfection.

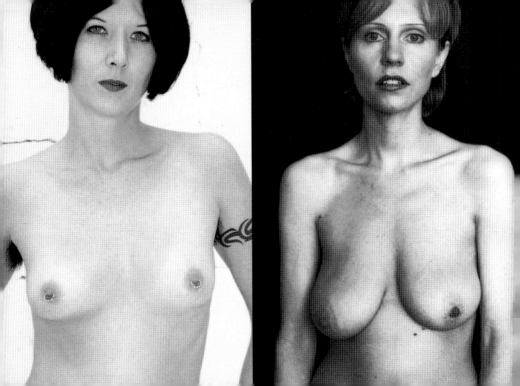

BEAUTY AND THE BREAST

From the real to the ideal may be a matter of centimeters, but it can occupy miles of head room. Ideals, too, come in many sizes and shapes, and the image-makers have offered up a host of breast

types. Each is perfect in its own way but highlights different feminine ideals. The breast that perfectly murmurs womanly warmth and sexiness (think Sophia Loren) is not the breast that declares stately, upper-crusty magnanimity (think Margaret Dumont). From an ideal of youth as pristine and untouched (or youth as free and sexually alert) to an ideal of motherhood, each has a breast shape to match.

There's room enough in our cluttered cultural landscape for multiple breast ideals, but different sizes and shapes have risen as the standard of beauty at certain times, from the apple-shaped breast of the Italian Renaissance to the bullet-shaped breast of the 1950s.

⬤ TIME PLUS GRAVITY   If the ages of man are represented by changes in posture, for women, the sagging breast tells time's story.

NAKED TRUTH   The difference between the real and the ideal can also be thought of as the difference between the "naked" and the "nude," as art historian Kenneth Clark has argued. While the naked person is portrayed as an unidealized bare body, the nude appears flawless, almost depersonalized. Manet's nude picnicker in *Déjeuner sur l'herbe* is at ease among her clothed companions— she's wearing a mask of perfection. In Wyeth's *Seated Nude*, the woman is both "naked" and lovely; her heavy breasts are as beautiful as they are true.

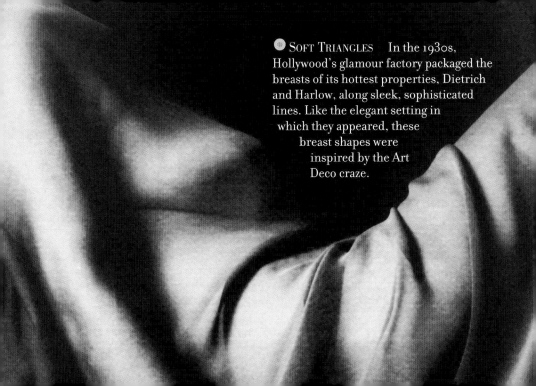

SOFT TRIANGLES In the 1930s, Hollywood's glamour factory packaged the breasts of its hottest properties, Dietrich and Harlow, along sleek, sophisticated lines. Like the elegant setting in which they appeared, these breast shapes were inspired by the Art Deco craze.

● THE STATUESQUE MARIANNE was born as a splendid national symbol during the French Revolution and was made into an icon in Delacroix's famous painting *Liberty Leading the People.* Recent incarnations have been modeled after glamorous figures like Brigitte Bardot, Catherine Deneuve and Ines de la Fressange. Marianne's shifting bust-line amply illustrates the changing ideals of the female breast.

1985: Deneuve as Marianne

1920s: Liberty as Flapper
Her slimmed-down bust embodies the postwar ideal of boyish freedom.

1940s: Marianne at Midcentury
Sporting a patriotic tricolor gown, her pointy breasts are torpedoes in France's arsenal.

1960s: Bardot as Marianne
Her presilicone beauties are the ripe (and visibly nippled) assets of a good-time girl.

STANDARD MODELS

Like an old standard reinterpreted by today's chanteuse, favored breast shapes resurface again and again. In these pairings, different artists from different eras come to the same conclusion: certain kinds of breasts are just plain beautiful.

EMERGING FROM WATER, this bathing beauty has breasts so plump and fleshy they seem ready to melt away.

ALPHA BREASTS are proud, taut
and firm, gravity-defying or
sloped for a slow dive.

● ANCIENT CLEOPATRA'S BREASTS fit her regal profile; Picasso's Madeleine has the same profile, expressed with liquid melancholy.

● PERFECT HANDFULS Like a peripatetic troupe of acclaimed actors, these bosom types are welcome in any country. Button nipples are the star attraction.

Cleopatra from the Temple of Dendera

Pablo Picasso, Woman in a Chemise, *1905*

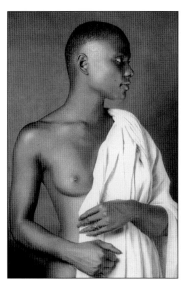

Hedy Lamarr in Ecstasy, *1933*   *Robert Mapplethorpe,* Ada, *1982*   *Shinsui,* October, *1929*

WORLDS APART These breasts seem to be making a bid for escape—from each other. With their almost cavernous cleavage, the breasts on Michelangelo's *Night* (right) have the air of add-ons (he used male models in keeping with convention and with his own sexual proclivities). Though the breasts of the Italian Venus are more integrated, she's being pulled apart—either by the male assistants grabbing her cloak or by the force of her breasts' perfect circularity.

Left, Trono Ludovisi,
Birth of Venus

● FASHION FIRST   Changes in clothing styles have a decided effect on how women feel about their breasts—and whether or not to disguise or enhance what they've got. While some contend that fashion follows a period's preference for breast type and shape, art historian Anne Hollander insists it's the other way around—our clothing has always called the shots. When long-waisted dresses were the fashion, so was the long-waisted nude; when styles emphasized the high-seated, far-apart bosom, as in Goya's wittily paired portraits, painted nudes followed suit.

Francisco de Goya y Lucientes,
The Clothed Maja *(left) and*
The Nude Maja *(above)*

Sweet Nothings

For centuries, a beautiful female body meant curves and softness (no matter that being fat meant you could afford to eat). Bones were considered unsightly, and breasts added yet more squeezability to the rounded form. In the 1920s came a sea change as women disencumbered themselves in all kinds of ways and sharp angles became prominent. In recent decades, wealth has meant you can afford *not* to eat, and in certain circles breasts have receded, the smaller the better.

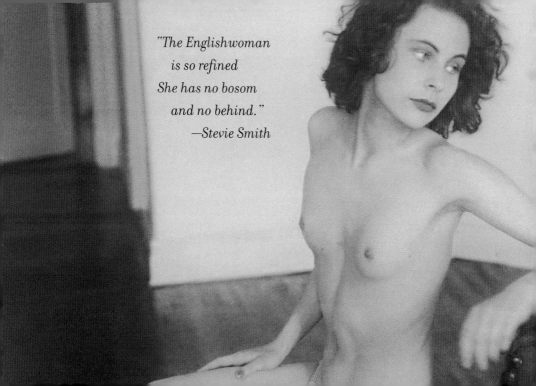

"The Englishwoman
is so refined
She has no bosom
and no behind."
—Stevie Smith

● SMALL, PERT BREASTS are forever young. In London's swinging sixties, youth was given the key to the city. British fashion icon Twiggy was flat-chested even by model standards. Looking great in a shift dress, her simplified physique also shifted emphasis from her breasts to her eyes (in little-girl fashion), with their signature false lashes and painted lower lids.

"It's not what you'd call a figure, is it?"
—Twiggy

PREHISTORIC BEAUTIES

Unearthed by archaeologists in the Austrian town of Willendorf in 1908, this Stone Age figure (c. 23,000 B.C.) could be a fertility goddess, the abstracted and distilled essence of womanhood, or it might have been modeled on a real woman. Some historians have insisted on the unlikelihood that Stone Age women could commonly have achieved so much girth, given the rigors of hunting down food; perhaps the uncommonness of corpulence made it all the more appealing.

Decades after its discovery, the figure was mockingly named the Venus of Willendorf. A more current (1966) version of Stone Age woman (and her distinctly unstony breasts) is represented in *One Million Years B.C.* with Raquel Welch as the Venus of L.A.

● BREAST-WISE, this Neolithic statuette (c. 3000 B.C.) and Makonde body mask (right) suggest the contours of an older woman (as Phyllis Diller joked, "My mother-in-law had a pain beneath her left breast—turned out to be a trick knee"). This interpretation, however, may be false; as Natalie Angier writes: "We erroneously associate floppy breasts with older breasts when in fact . . . some women's breasts are low-slung from the start."

Far right: The Himba tribe of Namibia valorizes youth—as in this young woman's spectacular breasts—though they also venerate old age.

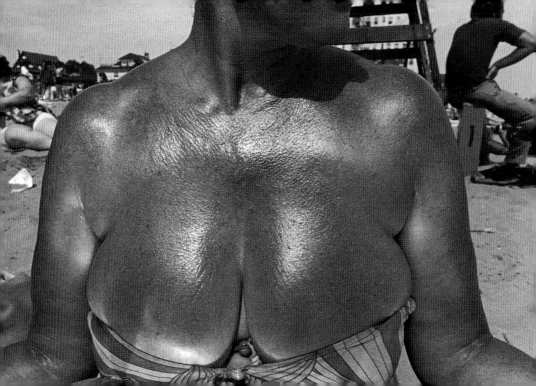

HEAVY-DUTY BREASTS speak for themselves, expressing a playful grandeur. Though this is not a breast type commonly admired today, these women would have been goddesses in the Paleolithic period. Even now they enjoy throwing their weight around.

THE SHAPE OF THINGS TO COME

The future, as we often imagine it, is a place where all things are orderly, regularized and hygienic (if not positively sterile), and breasts are no exception. Mass-produced on both women and robots, jutting out from under space suits or welded onto tin frames, these breasts are impossibly high, thrusting forward a step further in time. Breasts are *the* secondary sexual characteristic of the future, their round-ness suggesting not softness or nurturance but, like the sleek curves of fifties-era Cadillacs, powerful engines of seduction.

Far right,
Jane Fonda
in Barbarella,
1968

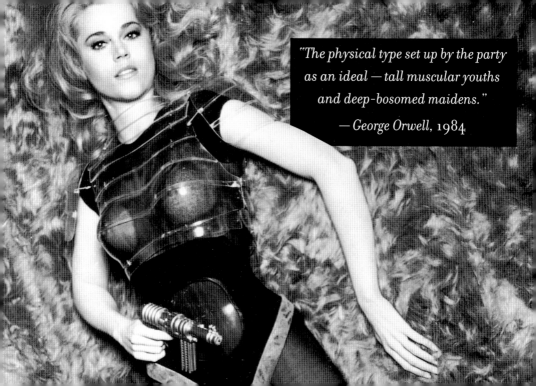

"The physical type set up by the party as an ideal — tall muscular youths and deep-bosomed maidens."

— George Orwell, 1984

TO EACH HER OWN

After the bickering of adolescence, a compromise is struck between a woman and her breasts, but she often continues to harbor an idea about the breasts she *should* have been given. By whatever mysterious logic she comes to favor one version over another, each woman has her personal paragon—maybe the polar opposite of her own, or hers with only

Édouard Manet, Brunette with Naked Breasts

minor adjustments. Some version of her ideal breasts is out there in the world—and she may encounter them on a stranger or, worse, a friend. Our ideas of what makes a breast beautiful—various and sometimes incongruous—are as distinctive and unaccountable as personality itself.

When Charlotte Brontë immortalized the plain heroine in *Jane Eyre*, whose beauty of soul was not reflected in her visage, she expressed the feelings of countless women: Why can't our appearance reflect the best in our character? Why, we might add, can't our breasts reflect the compass of our souls?

A Feast for the Eyes

"The babe, emerging from its liquid bed,
Now lifts in gelid air its nodding head . . .
Seeks with spread hands the bosom's velvet orbs,
With closing lips the milky fount absorbs . . ."
—Anonymous

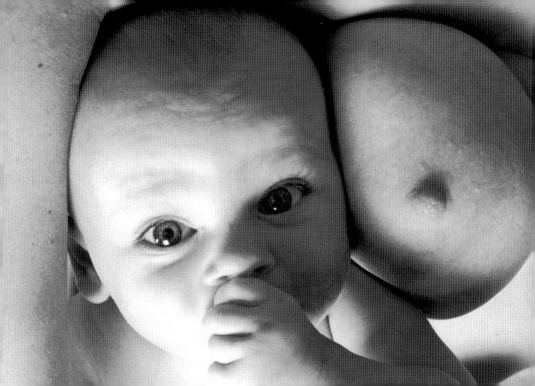

Can we remember what it first felt like to see a breast—up close? Perhaps even before we look into our mother's eyes, we dive instinctively for the breast, in part because our just-opened eyes are drawn to concentric circles. Faced with this bull's-eye of satisfaction and satiation, bigger than our own head, we zoom in. And even if our mother isn't sure how to offer her breasts (and if, in later life, we ourselves stumble over the first nursing),

the baby can be the teacher. We're born with the instinct to suck—and with muscles that allow for some powerful and determined suckling. Right from the start we know how and where to feed.

GOT MILK? Babies tuck in to the best food they can eat—their perfect diet for the first few months.

ORAL HISTORY

Breasts loom large in the psychic imagination, and first feedings point to the beginning of our fascination. Dubbing the pleasure of suckling "oral-eroticism," psychologists have found a wealth of connections between the development of

later emotional life and our first experiences at the breast. Breast-feeding isn't just about the passage of liquid from breast to mouth; it also engages the nerves, including those of the mother, who may herself experience a subtle erotic pleasure. Some have called suckling a kind of ur-pleasure that later sexual activity aims to recapture. Child psychoanalyst D.W. Winnicott has suggested that when breast-feeding goes well, a baby feels that its feeding has created the breast. Reliably appearing as hunger mounts, the breast becomes both an independent object and the creation of our imagination and desire, shaping our world view.

Left, Picasso, Maternité, 1905; right, Woody Allen's Everything You Always Wanted to Know About Sex, 1972

MAKING MILK

*"It is pleasant when a part of
your body makes sense, after
all these years."*
—Anne Enright

Typically, a woman lives with her breasts for quite some time, fine-tuning her relationship with them, before she finds out what they can do. Her breasts lie quietly in wait, standing armies of ducts and lobules, prepared long ahead of time for milk production. Underneath the first swellings of pubescence (and the only forgivable fatty tissue), the mammary glands have developed into firm, rubbery lobes and ducts that will produce and channel the milk to the nipple's surface. Each breast usually has five to nine lobes; from each one there flows a delicate network of lactiferous ducts that function as intricately as a master computer. The ducts perforate the skin of the nipple, forming tiny holes. In the course of nursing, the nipple functions much like the spout of a watering can.

Right, Jayne Mansfield in The Girl Can't Help It, *1956*

In pregnancy, breasts can take on a life of their own, changing almost as radically in size and shape as during puberty. They grow bigger (by as much as a pound while producing milk) and change their look: the areola darkens and spreads, sometimes to a shockingly different shape and color. These new breasts, though, are only temporary; after the baby is weaned, they retract (more or less) on cue to their former state: the lobules atrophy, the ducts regress and the areola reduces. Permanent changes in size

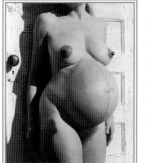

or shape are usually the result not of breast-feeding but of pregnancy itself, though even an informed starlet like Patricia Arquette was quoted otherwise: "Me and my friends who breast-fed make fun of our breasts. We say they're now more like figs. Or like a scarf!"

Our bodily urges (most infamously, the sex drive) are governed mainly by hormones, and lactation is no exception. Just after birth, the body releases prolactin into the bloodstream to initiate lactation, and as long as suckling continues, this hormone remains active. Prolactin can also be generated by the act of suckling, which has enabled some adoptive mothers to breast-feed. Oxytocin, the hormone that controls the let-down reflex, can be triggered simply by *thinking* about one's new baby or even by the cries of another child. This can mean the accidental flow that nursing mothers call "spilt milk in the supermarket"—a damp shirt from hearing a baby's wail in another aisle.

NIPPLE NUMMERARY

We think of our two breasts as a natural twinning, but in fact the number of breasts and nipples is governed by a more abstract law— the average number of progeny produced in a single birthing. According to one theory, the number of mammaries is usually twice the average litter size (in humans, just one). An estimated 1 percent of the human population breaks the rule, with either polythelia (extra nipples) or polymastia (extra breast tissue).

Previous page, Imogen Cunningham, Pregnant Nude, *1959; left, Ivory Coast statue*

*Nipple shield,
1545–1830*

Silver nipple shield, 1829

*Silver nipple protector,
1751*

*Lead shield,
1634*

● NIPPLE SHIELDS protect the suckling nipple from rawness, soreness, or just plain overuse. The nipple is self-lubricating thanks to oil glands on its surface, but sometimes a little help is welcome—particularly since it no longer comes in the form of metal or wood.

*Wooden nipple shield,
1830*

SUCKLING SENSATIONS

The experience of breast-feeding, before it happens, often seems unimaginable. If and when you finally do breast-feed, the *feeling* may be entirely different from what you had expected. Some women find it the apex of bliss, forging an intimate connection with their child. Others experience it as painful (many breasts chafe or just become sore), awkward or uncomfortable; some, in fact, find the experience so unpleasurable that even though their intention was to breast-feed for the first year (as doctors now recommend), they stop after a few weeks or months.

Routinely, the act of breast-feeding is a revelation. As Anne Enright addressed breast-feeding in her diary: "So let's call it nursing and let's be discreet—it's still the best way I know to clear a room. My breast (left or right, whichever is at issue) is not the problem, the 'problem' is the noise. Sometimes a child drinks as simply as from a cup, other times she snorts and gulps, half-drowns, sputters and gasps;

Right, Paula Modersohn-Becker, Mother and Child Lying Nude, 1907

then she squawks a bit, and starts all over again. This may be an iconized activity made sacred by some and disgusting by others, but it is first and foremost a meal. It is only occasionally serene."

"One of the greatest unexpected pleasures of breast-feeding is how it slows down time.
The zen of motherhood: eight to ten times a day, you get to kick back and let down."
—Kate T. Morgan

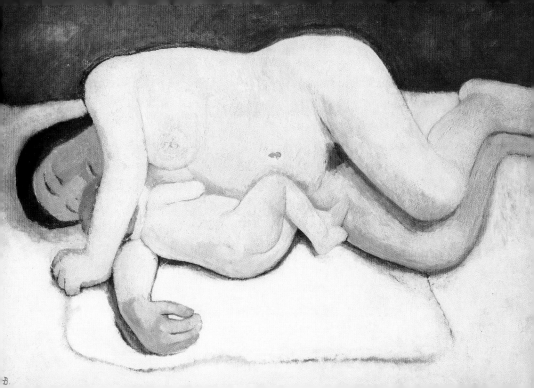

BREAST IS BEST

We still don't understand the exact composition of breast milk—another testament to the body's mystifying complexity. But it is baby's perfect food, containing over 100 components, including defenders against allergies, viruses and germs. We also know that breast milk varies from mother to mother and according to the baby's needs; the milk of premature babies' mothers contains fats particularly suited to their fragile digestive systems.

Breast cells during lactation

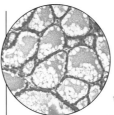

Breast cells at rest

Breast-feeding benefits the mother, too. Besides accelerating the contraction of the uterus to its prepregnancy proportions, breast-feeding helps shed the extra weight gained during pregnancy, burning an extra 500 to 1,000 calories a day. Recent studies show that women who breast-feed have lower rates of breast, ovarian and uterine cancer and osteoporosis. And since it suppresses ovulation, breast-feeding can also be a natural contraceptive.

In a world without formula, a plentiful supply of breast milk was essential to the infant's survival, and special potions were prescribed to nursing mothers. Some of these had real medicinal value—increasing

the mother's fluid content—but others seem closer to witchcraft. Romans urged new mothers to swallow earthworms with honeyed wine or dilute the ashes of bats in water and rub the paste on their chests. One

Leaflike structures of milk-secreting glands within the breast

sixteenth-century British formula reads like a recipe for chicken soup, except it calls for powder of earthworms and tongue of newt.

WHITE BLOOD

For much of history, breast milk was believed to originate in body parts other than the breasts. Ancient Greeks believed that it was not milk at all but "white blood," menstrual blood diverted in pregnancy to the growing fetus and after birth to the breasts—where it lost its crimson color. Many early cultures forbade nursing mothers to have intercourse to prevent semen from souring their milk.

OTHER THAN MOTHER:
WET-NURSING

Though it might seem strange today to have children feeding at the breasts of women other than their mothers, surrogate breast-feeding has a long history. In peasant cultures, shared nursing was a natural part of life—and of the female community. Communal nursers allowed women to help one another if a mother fell ill, was unable to nurse or had multiple children of breast-feeding age. In the upper classes, surrogate nursing meant something else: you could afford to pay a wet nurse to breast-feed in your stead.

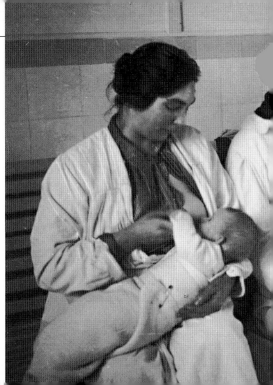

● THE ANCIENT WORLD used wet nurses, too. As infants, Moses and Muhammad were entrusted to surrogate mothers. (Unbeknownst to the pharaoh, Moses' wet nurse was his biological mother.) While most Egyptians, Babylonians and Hebrews breast-fed their children for about three years, the wealthy used slaves or others as wet nurses. (Under Islamic law, a boy and girl suckled by the same wet nurse are "milk sister and brother" and cannot be married.) In ancient Rome, philosophers debated the topic: Plato advocated wet-nursing, while Plutarch and Tacitus argued that the strong attachment between child and wet nurse might threaten the bond to the mother.

Left, ancient Egyptian wet nurse; right, Moses nursing

Despite Jonah's biblical admonishment, "even the sea monsters draw out the breast [and] give suck to their young," European women of wealth and status heeded their own, more pressing concerns—among them the fear that breast-feeding would ruin the shape of their delicate breasts. From the late Middle Ages on, most wealthy parents in Europe employed wet nurses as a sign of good breeding or class. As the practice expanded throughout the Continent, government bureaus were established in major cities to regulate and oversee the trade. In France, where wet-nursing proved most popular, even parents among the urban lower classes sent their babies to surrogate breast-feeders in country villages; in 1780, of 21,000 babies born in Paris, barely 1,000 were nursed by their mothers. (France also saw wet-nursing's latest demise. Even in the early twentieth century, 80,000 French babies were sent to wet nurses in the countryside.)

Étienne Jeaurat, Arrival of the Wet Nurses, *c. 1750s*

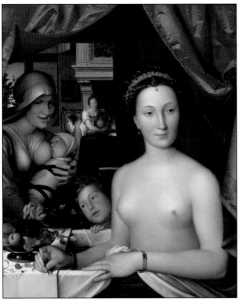

The royal "we" did not always include the babe at the breast. Queen Victoria was nursed by her mother, the Duchess of Kent, but declined to breast-feed her own nine children; her daughter Alice wrote the queen a long letter to justify her own decision to nurse her first child. Since breast-feeding was thought to be a natural contraceptive, wet-nursing may have been a way of assuring aristocrats of lineal descent. Multiple offspring were a hedge against shockingly high infant mortality rates, and new mothers among the nobility were whisked off to the matrimonial bed to ensure they would soon be pregnant again.

⬤ ROYAL RELIEF   The title Madame Poitrine (Mrs. Breast) was one of the perks enjoyed by women who wet-nursed French monarchs, although they were usually aristocrats themselves. Here, the haughty Dame Longuet de La Giraudière, wet nurse to the future Louis XIV, offers a bosom fit for a king.

PRIZE PAPS

Judith Waterford's remarkable fifty-year career as a wet nurse was recorded in medical journals in 1831. In her prime she could produce two quarts of milk a day, and on her eighty-first birthday she demonstrated that she could still squeeze "nice, sweet" milk from her left breast.

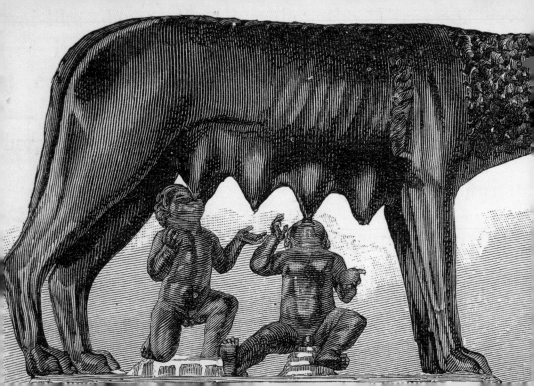

🐾 ROMULUS AND REMUS nursed at the breast of a she-wolf and survived to found Rome. While real-life attempts were made to have children nurse at the paps of animals, women in some cultures suckled puppies to relieve their engorged breasts.

NATURE OR NURTURE?

Before the science of genetics, breast milk was thought to transmit physical traits and personality from breast-feeder to breast-fed. For those who did not breast-feed their own children, choosing a wet nurse became a matter of great importance—a search to find the cream of the crop, so to speak.

Different methods were applied to prevent the baby from being "changed" by the wet nurse's milk. The mother might want a woman who resembled her or who had a child of the same gender (a wet nurse with a daughter might "feminize" a boy). In the

Middle Ages, if you were Jewish and your wet nurse was Christian, you would ask her to spill her milk for three days after taking Easter Communion, since she'd just ingested the body of Christ.

Wet nurses were carefully examined beforehand and closely observed during their tenure. Since "goodness" might also be passed through milk, a wet nurse was expected to eat and live "right." The shape and texture of her breasts also made a difference. Rabelais, in the sixteenth century, attributed the beautiful nose of one of his characters to the soft

Honoré Daumier,
The Third-
Class Carriage

WET NURSE WANTED:

Good health a requisite; good teeth a selling point. During interview, nurse required to have her milk tasted for sweetness.

nipples of her wet nurse and observed that "wet nurses with hard nipples make snub-nosed babies." Hair color was another consideration: redheads' milk was thought to have an unpleasant smell, and brunettes were considered better milk providers than blonds. Even in the nineteenth century, Lady Margot Asquith recalled that her sister Charlotte was believed to be taller than the rest of the family as a result of her statuesque wet nurse.

We may call it a divine gift, but artistic talent was once believed to be passed on through breast milk. Michelangelo thought his gift for sculpting came from his wet nurse—a stonecutter's wife. "At the breast," he said, "I sucked in the hammers and chisels that I use for my statues."

MR. MOM

Men, in fact, possess the apparatus for producing milk but not the hormones that trigger its production. There is speculation today, however, that with hormonal treatments men might pitch in when it comes to breast-feeding. In 1884 the *British Medical Journal* reported that one sympathetic fellow was so upset by his wife's childbirth pains that he grew ill, took to his bed and began to secrete milk from his breast.

Right, Ambrogio Lorenzetti, Madonna del Latte, *c. 1300; far right, Veronese's* Mars and Venus *shows Venus squirting breast milk toward her son Cupid.*

HOLY MOTHER

I mages of this pretty pair have been represented as far back as recorded civilization, often in the form of goddesses nursing their divine offspring, though the most recognizable image is that of the Virgin Mary suckling the baby Jesus.

Called Maria Lactans (*lac* is Latin for milk), the earliest such image dates to the third century. The great flowering of paintings celebrating the Madonna and

Child came in the Middle Ages and early Renaissance. Demonstrating Mary's mercy through her powers of intercession and healing, they also showed the paradox of sublime humility as the son of God clung to the breast of his mortal mother.

 WHITE AND GLEAMING, the Virgin's milk was thought to be the earthly equivalent of astral light: a heavenly emanation. Vials believed to contain a few drops of Mary's milk were found as relics in churches throughout Europe, leading the skeptical John Calvin to write: "There is so much that if the holy Virgin had been a cow, or a wet nurse all her life, she would have been hard put to it to yield such a great quantity."

 SALUTARY DROPS of Mary's milk were aimed into the mouths of saints, visionaries, penitents, those stricken with disease and sufferers in Purgatory. Symbolic of the nurturing institution of the Church, her milk offered sustenance to the Christian soul.

Left, Leonardo da Vinci, The Little Madonna; above, the Virgin Mary feeding St. Bernard

By the fourteenth century, renderings of Maria Lactans became more domestic, emphasizing emotional bonding and leading the way for artists to take on the subject of breast-feeding as an image of sacred serenity for all mothers. Perhaps that's why even non-religious portraits of nursing mother and child still seem touched by a form of faith. This atmosphere of self-sustaining bliss (in which the giver is perpetually replenished) conveys the miracle at hand: a mother, for the brief window of infancy, can satisfy *all*.

Left, Luca Loughi,
Maria Lactans;
right, Jan Gossaert,
Madonna and child

BABY JESUS has been depicted with breasts, but such role reversals of mother and child were intended as allegories for the nurturing power of the Savior.

PUBLIC INTEREST

Different cultures have at different times tried to regulate the practice of breast-feeding through suggestive policies, incentives and even the law. During the French Revolution, mothers were required to breast-feed in order to receive stipends from the government. At the turn of the nineteenth century, German women were paid premiums for breast-feeding their children, a practice continued today in French-speaking Quebec.

Later, in Nazi-era Germany, Aryan women were required to breast-feed at regular intervals and (in keeping with the Nazi zeal for record keeping) to undergo tests to establish exactly how much milk they were producing. In Paris, from the 1930s to early '40s, a center was established where milk donors were paid to supply breast milk as a "medicine" for infants in need. And in present-day Tasmania mothers

Left, Leon Frederic, The Age of the Worker; *right, Martine Franck, working mother nursing*

are required to sign a consent form if they want to give baby formula to their infants.

The advent of baby formula in the mid-nineteenth century altered the course of breast-feeding history; by 1940, only 25 percent of American mothers were breast-feeding. Movements like La Leche League have subsequently sought to reintroduce breast-feeding and its benefits, with some success, and many countries have even enacted pro-breast-feeding policies. According to the World Health Organization, 21 of 31 countries in Africa, 22 of 25 countries in Latin America, 14 of 17 countries in the eastern Mediterranean, and 21 of 35 countries in Europe have formal breast-feeding policies.

Currently in the United States, 60 percent of women who leave the hospital with their newborn are breast-feeding, with only 21 percent still at it six months later. (The Surgeon General's goal is to make that 75 percent.)

Nestlé's advertisement c. 1890 claims healthier babies through formula.

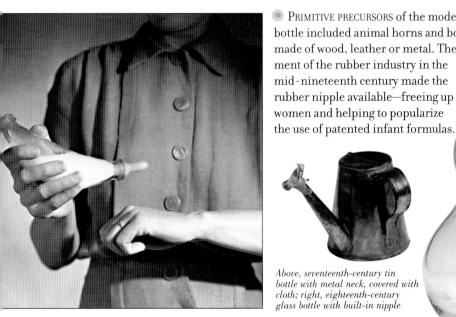

PRIMITIVE PRECURSORS of the modern baby bottle included animal horns and bottles made of wood, leather or metal. The development of the rubber industry in the mid-nineteenth century made the rubber nipple available—freeing up women and helping to popularize the use of patented infant formulas.

Above, seventeenth-century tin bottle with metal neck, covered with cloth; right, eighteenth-century glass bottle with built-in nipple

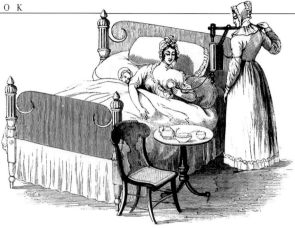

● BUSY MOTHERS (working or not) have relied on breast pumps (or "breast exhausters") to stockpile milk for those occasions when they have to be elsewhere at feeding time. Some hands-free devices (right) allow new moms to nurse mechanically while they're out and about.

PUBLIC ACCESS

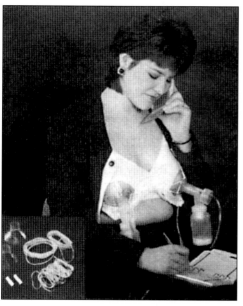

Breast-feeding in public was, for much of history, a perfectly common and natural sight. Where did we go wrong? In recent decades, particularly in the United States, public nursing has been problematic. In 1975 three women in a Miami park were arrested for indecent exposure while nursing their infants, an event that in effect classified breast-feeding with other forms of sexual exposure. Duration of breast-feeding has also caused contention since some view nursing past toddlerhood as unnatural. While experts estimate that the average weaning age worldwide today is three years old, in the United States and some European countries a serious stigma is attached to prolonged breast-feeding. (Recently an Illinois mother temporarily lost custody of her five-year-old son after a baby-sitter phoned an abuse hot line and reported that the child was still being breast-fed.)

Perhaps it is our predominantly sexualized view of the breast that has stigmatized child-led weaning, the suspicion that, like for Toni Morrison's Ruth in *Song of Solomon* (whose school-age son earns the nickname Milkman because he goes home at lunch to nurse), the practice becomes the mother's "secret indulgence." *She* is the one who does not want to be weaned. Still, recent legislation has sought to make life for the breast-feeding mother feasible. In 1994, New York State amended the civil rights law to grant mothers the right to breast-feed in public; and to date twenty other states have followed suit.

Mary Ellen Mark, 1980. Breast-feeding in public enables women to take motherhood on the road; in this case, baby seems to be multitasking, too.

THE SHADOW
OF YOUNG GIRLS IN BLOOM

"Tis true, your budding Miss is very charming,
But shy and awkward at first coming out,
So much alarm'd that she is quite alarming,
All Giggle, Blush: half Pertness, and half Pout."
—*Anonymous*

One day: an explosion. Whether anticipated or feared, the beginning of puberty is as unsettling as a seismic shift—an earthquake where once the ground was firm. With her hormones erupting, a girl's growth rate accelerates. (Boys' growth spurts come later.) Angular or round, awkward or self-possessed, her new body may be the one secret she can't keep. Though all girls go through the collective experience of maturing, they do so in single file, each at her own rate—and true to her own form.

We're on Our Way: Some girls are ready as toddlers, while others are children up to the brink.

POINTING THE WAY

From the flat freedom of girlhood, a sprouting begins. Breast buds—the puffing and thickening of breast

tissue just behind the areolae that make the nipples literally bloom— develop on average two years before a girl's first period. Usually somewhere between the ages of eight and thirteen, the brain dissemi- nates gonadotropin-releasing hormones (GnRH), which in turn stimulate the pituitary gland to release two key puberty hormones, luteinizing hormone (LH) and follicle-stimulating hormone (FSH); these travel to the ovaries and stimulate estrogen production. In an endocrinal chorus, the body readies for motherhood, however distant it may be, by widening the pelvis, preparing the uterus, and developing the fat and mammary glands that will become breasts.

Left, young woman, Ivory Coast; right, Sally Mann, Scarlett Nipples

"A body part that we didn't start out with—Whole new organs, two of them, tricky to hide or eradicate, attached for all the world to see."
—Francine Prose

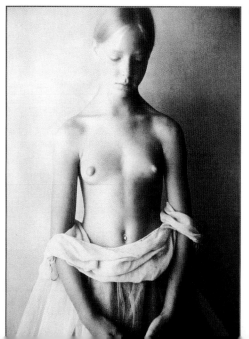

AN EIGHT-YEAR-OLD WOMAN   Precocious puberty has attracted a great deal of publicity. While the average age for the onset of puberty has historically been eleven years (the standard from a study in the 1960s), recent reports set the average closer to ten years. Reasons cited for early sexual maturity include the effect of cow's milk (and bovine growth hormone), estrogen stimulators in foods such as chicken or even airborne in our environment, and, oddly enough, some studies show that the absence of a father can activate hormones. Weight in particular has long been known to affect maturation: overweight girls develop earlier; underweight girls develop later.

THE FIRST DAY OF THE REST OF YOUR LIFE

Your first kiss, your first period, your first zit, your first bra—in the list of firsts, we've concocted the

hurdles that constitute the ascent to adolescence. These rites of passage not only introduce you to each particular experience, but as the first in a series of experiences, they open up a whole new universe. Growing up happens in several directions. In the seminal teen book *Are You There God? It's Me, Margaret*, one girl announces, with her chest thrust out, "I'm growing already—in a few years, I'm going to look like one of those girls in *Playboy*." When Margaret and her friends chant the childhood ditty "We must, we must, we must increase our bust!" and flex their arms, it's a race—and breasts will throw them over the finish line.

Left, Chardin,
Girl with Shuttlecock

⬤ ANTICIPATION   Little girls know they're coming. They may have spent part of their early life eyeing breasts—face to face, so to speak—and now they want their own. In dress-up games, they stuff objects of all shapes and sizes into their shirts, from tennis balls to oranges to the proverbial sock, in order to play grown-up.

"GIRL, YOU'RE A WOMAN NOW."

A young girl's first trip to the lingerie department is a heady, telescoped vision of what's in store. In the quiet rows of satin, cotton, nylon and silk, she sees her breasts and her future identities unfold—from the lacy numbers of seduction to the nursing bras of motherhood to the extra-support contraptions of maturity. There, with the help of that old hand, the professional saleswoman, she receives a neat letter and number code—her first measure of femininity.

The first bra is usually a training bra, more a bra-in-waiting than the real thing.

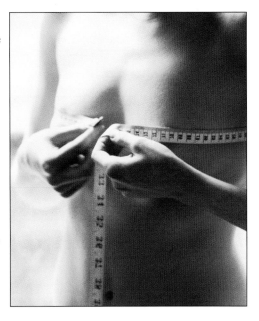

The novel idea of "training" the bosom dates from the 1950s. Before then, girls wore "waists," or camisoles, fitted undershirts without cups or darts, then moved to adult bras when they could fill them. But in the fifties, along with the commodification of everything, bra manufacturers (aided and abetted by the medical profession) began looking at the teen market. With new fun names like Gro-Bra, Bobbie and Adagio, these "teen-proportioned" undergarments came in

double- or triple-A sizes, catering more to the wish for breasts than their actual appearance. In the decade that invented the juvenile delinquent card, girls were admonished to exert "junior figure control," and these proto-brassieres were preparing them for a life of moral restraint.

As the teen demographic proved successful, bra manufacturers began making films to illustrate the necessity of "proper" undergarments. Shown in home economics classrooms across the country, films with titles like *Facts About Your Figure* trained generations of girls to put their faith in brassieres as a form of social control—

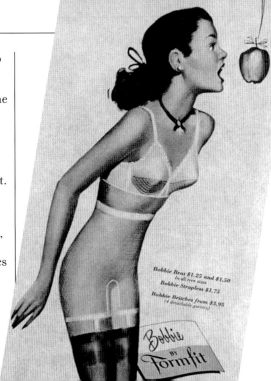

Bobbie Bras $1.25 and $1.50
In all true sizes
Bobbie Strapless $1.75

Bobbie Britches from $3.95
(4 detachable garters)

Bobbie
by
Formfit

whether shaping the bosom or saying "Hands off."

Trained, readied and strapped in, these first breasts probably won't be the last. Some breasts come in at full size, others begin small and suddenly swell in late adolescence, still others stay the same size from first blush. Even if you remain the same weight your whole life, your breasts can change size—again and again. (Some breasts change size later in life. Some shrink after pregnancy; others grow.)

In the 1950s, training bras were a fixture of adolescence.

NOT JUST A GIRL THING

Did you know that both male and female embryos develop "milk ridges" in utero at about ten to fifteen weeks? These two strips of tissue run from the armpit over the chest and down the stomach. Later these milk ridges regress, leaving just two nipples. But sometime during adolescence, about 65 percent of "normal" boys experience breast development (on at least one side). Known as gynecomastia, male breast development is usually self-limiting and disappears over a period of months. Causes include hormonal irregularities, marijuana usage and certain medications.

JUST A PHASE

Our idea of adolescence as a distinct phase between childhood and adulthood is relatively recent. Some cultural historians and anthropologists trace it to the nineteenth century;

others, like Margaret Mead in her trendsetting *Coming of Age in Samoa*, argue that adolescence as we

Left, Papuan girl has assumed the adult role of warrior; right, girls in French Guiana

now think of it—as a time of social and sexual conflict, resolution and passage to the adult world—is a culturally specific phenomenon. Indeed, some cultures do not experience it as a distinct phase at all.

Interestingly, Freud did not view adolescence as a particularly fertile period of psychosexual development. He believed that early childhood experiences were the formative basis of later sexual development and that adolescent conflicts were simply replaying childhood dynamics. More recently, psychology has explored the ways in which body image develops in the formative period of adolescence, particularly in

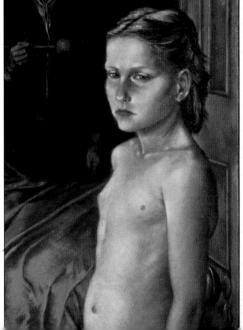

relation to teenage anorexia and bulimia. (Some psychologists interpret anorexia as a willed arresting of development. The acute loss of weight puts all signs of puberty on hold—with the cessation of menstruation or the diminishing of breasts.) Most current research has looked at adolescence as the breeding ground for psychosexual conditioning; if sexuality can be problematic for adults, just think how much more troubling it can be for girls making the transition into their new bodies and new selves.

Moody Youth: *left, Dorothea Tanning,* The Friend's Room; *right, Edvard Munch,* Puberty

SELF-SCRUTINY

O mirror, mirror on the wall. Mirrors lighten, enlarge and reflect, enhancing the state into which adolescents fall most easily: self-contemplation. Most adolescent girls' bedrooms are equipped with a mirror, whether handheld, over a vanity or inside a closet, and around the litter of discarded clothing, behind closed doors, they spend hours dressing, checking and examining. They may practice a kiss on the mirror; in some ways, adolescent girls conduct their best love affairs with

Alone or in groups, girls study themselves. Right, Balthus, Nude in Profile.

"I have often noticed that when women look at themselves in every reflection, and take furtive peeps into their hand looking-glasses, it is hardly ever, as is generally supposed, from vanity, but much more often from a feeling that all is not quite as it should be."
—Nancy Mitford,
The Pursuit of Love

themselves—though an imaginary partner may be hiding behind the glass.

There's so much to think about when everything is changing, and an acute feeling of self-consciousness is the normal state of affairs. For the first time, the adolescent may feel that her body is composed of discrete parts—each with its own message, hankering for her attention. She's also exploring what it means to have this new body: whether she likes it, what it feels like, or whether she would perhaps like a different one. Rumors are rampant: Does being flat mean you're sexless? Does having big breasts mean you're easy?

Hopefully, these judgments are passed quietly or kept in reserve. For whether, like Jamaica Kincaid, you saw your breasts' beginnings as "treasured shrubs, needing only the proper combination of water and sunlight to make them flourish" or hid them under an extra-large T-shirt, coming to terms with new breasts is a remarkably individual process. In the mirror's shifting surface, you're being reborn.

NEITHER THIS NOR THAT

Adolescence can be a kind of limbo—a state of contained but perpetual change. Not only is your body morphing on an almost daily basis, but the world around you is mirroring its transformations. For the first time, an adolescent girl may turn heads or stop traffic; certainly, depending on the way in which she develops, she will be teased or whistled at, ogled or pinched, or have her bra strap pulled. Half child, half adult, caught between the familiar and the strange, the adolescent is mired in a quicksand of questioning—aided by hormones that trigger impulses, moody and sexual.

● CAUGHT IN THE MIDDLE   Looking head-on or looking away, awkward in each decision, the adolescent is in a state of mutation.

● ENVIABLE YOUTH Adolescence can also seem to be a time of enormous freedom. Using explosions of energy to propel them up, down or chest forward, girls may revel in their longer reach.

● NEVER-NEVER LAND   This paradigm
of girl-boyhood is literally stopped at the
brink—frozen at the moment before gender
starts to take over. Peter Pan, tribal leader of
children who never grow up, is traditionally
played by a woman (though one whose
breasts are bound to prepubescence), pro-
viding a fantasy for both boys and girls want-
ing freedom from adults and adulthood. This
Peter Pan is Hayley Mills, a teen star who
retained the innocence of childhood—and
breastlessness—in her roles.

● "LOOK AT ME. I'M LIKE DEFORMED."   In
Slums of Beverly Hills, thirteen-year-old
Vivian looks in the mirror at her new
breasts—and they're big. As her father says,
"It happened, I tell you, overnight. She got
stacked, just like her mother."

JAILBAIT

In these complicated times, images of adolescent girls often become fodder for moral outrage. Portraits of young girls' budding sexuality magnify the ambiguity of their "dreamy childishness and eerie vulgarity," as Vladimir Nabokov put it in the censored *Lolita*. For some, these portraits reflect

a culture so sexualized that its youth has been corrupted. Whether such images reveal the inherent sexuality of young women or their subjects being sexualized—unbeknownst to them or, worse, under coercion—begs troubling questions about personal, sexual and political boundaries. (One alarming theory about precocious puberty suggests that a hypersexualized environment is overstimulating girls to develop early.) Conversely, in our youth-oriented culture, the development of a womanly figure sometimes seems frowned upon. Mothers dress to look like teenage girls; Madonna admires (and wants to collaborate with) Britney Spears. And many models have bodies that appear hauntingly prepubescent—or they are themselves just entering puberty.

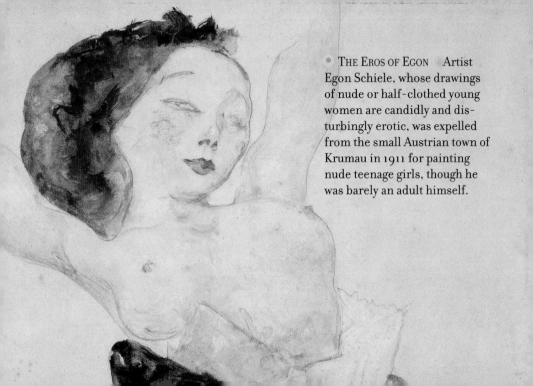

THE EROS OF EGON   Artist Egon Schiele, whose drawings of nude or half-clothed young women are candidly and disturbingly erotic, was expelled from the small Austrian town of Krumau in 1911 for painting nude teenage girls, though he was barely an adult himself.

What is clear is the striking and innate beauty of the best of these images. The paradox, if viewed with empathy, is not necessarily between the objectified child and the sexualizing (and adult) audience, but between the child and the woman within the girl—her own conflicted sense of power and innocence. At its best, this genre ably captures the ambivalence with which we come of age and with which we are regarded by the world around us. As young girls toy with sexuality, onlookers turn squeamish because they know too well how treacherous this path to adulthood can be.

● NERVOUS ABOUT NYMPHETS For both movie versions of *Lolita*, the casting of the title role rattled nerves. For the British version, Sue Lyon (right) was chosen (at the censor's demand) because she was of age and looked to be more adult than child, like a china doll with full-grown breasts. At the right age, and therefore prohibited by law from performing the sex scenes, Dominique Swain (above) was probably closer to Nabokov's conception of an underdeveloped coquette: careless, awkward and not quite filled out.

CELLULOID BABIES

Most girls come of age in the relative privacy of the home, but young stars of television and screen must blossom in full view. Some ease into adolescence by possessing a kind of preternatural sexuality; others fall afoul of the public by betraying its desire to have them be forever innocent. Many become icons of transition with all the attendant pain and frustration.

SHIRLEY TEMPLE, the dimpled, curly-mopped box-office champion of the 1930s and '40s, is still the world's favorite little girl. Though she came into herself becomingly, with a full chest and wavy hair, audiences never quite forgave her for growing up. As Shirley Temple Black, she reentered public life as a congresswoman and an ambassador. She was also one of the first public figures to announce that she'd had a mastectomy and to urge women to have regular mammograms.

DEANNA DURBIN was a star as a teenager, albeit one who had the good graces to behave like a child. Young, innocent and good-natured, like Mickey Rooney, she was a beloved staple of films like *One Hundred Men and a Girl* and *That Certain Age*. Deanna's first screen kiss made newspaper headlines, but she did not survive the transition to adulthood. Featured next to an outsized vase of pussy willows in this picture, she looks dwarfed into childhood—though her pockets may be concealing something else.

BROOKE SHIELDS began her acting career as a child prostitute whose innocent appearance troublingly intensified her erotic appeal. After a series of sexy roles in teen successes like *Blue Lagoon* and Madison Avenue's "Nothing comes between me and my Calvins," she declared her commitment to premarital celibacy. She became America's First Virgin—the most famous since Doris Day.

JODIE FOSTER, as a streetwise girl prostitute in *Taxi Driver*, wore tarted-up clothes that sat awkwardly on her pubescent figure. Interestingly, she's managed the transition to adulthood by taking powerful roles that desex her or call for more conservative clothes—and by taking the reins as a director and producer.

Beach Blanket Bingo, *1965*

TEEN QUEEN

At the top of teenage culture is the teen queen—the girl who, whether cheerleader or honor student, seems to take adolescence in stride. Teen queens don't acknowledge their stage of development; they let their full breasts announce it for them. As the ones who have best assumed adult roles, they're infallible, fully formed. They take their breasts on parade, status symbols of their invulnerability.

If teen culture celebrates the giddiness of youth, much of it is spent trying to accelerate past awkwardness. For most girls, this involves the first sexual fumblings. After all these growing pains, breasts turn out to be erogenous zones—the first stop on the sexual freeway.

● BEACH BALL Annette Funicello, sweetheart of the Mickey Mouse Club, ballooned into the hearts and imaginations of young TV viewers. This teen queen was the perfect model for the new two-piece bathing suit—bouffant in more ways than one.

● I'M NOT SO INNOCENT! When Britney sings of accidentally breaking hearts—as in "Oops, I Did It Again"—we know she's just playing grown-up. Like her alleged breast implants, she's putting us on; her aerobic gyrations mimic sex—without having it.

SHAPING THE SILHOUETTE

"On the soft wax of the human body, each society stamps its imprint."
—*Philippe Perrot*

At the front line of aesthetic and erotic appeal, breasts have always pushed fashion forward, shaping the ideal female form. But no one body part acts alone; a woman's curves collaborate to form a kind of whole that we call the figure, trained under the often tough tutelage of lingerie—as when corsets were tightened to achieve an hourglass silhouette. Enhancing or restricting, fitting the form to the fashion of the day, lingerie has always offered itself up to make the ideal real by creating the perfect silhouette.

Nineteenth-century cartoon parodies fashion's way with nature.

SECOND SKIN

It's amazing what you can achieve when you take two breasts and apply a little pressure or padding. Squeezing or binding, firming or flattening, pushing up or filling out, a woman's bra molds and sculpts her bosom. Working with the boundless natural variety of shapes and sizes, bras can improve upon nature (they aren't called Miracle Bras for nothing!) by pressing breasts into conformity or emphazing their glorious differences. And unlike plastic surgery, sculpting the bosom is a *temporary* art form, allowing a woman to arrange her breasts in different ways at

*Naomi Campbell knows
what a bra can do.*

different times to make a multitude of personal statements.

Simple physical comfort did not become a value in female undergarments until the twentieth century. In certain periods, physical immobility was considered a luxury, and servants would dress and undress you. The modern bra, the first attempt at over-the-shoulder breast support, was an invention of the modern mind. The word *brassiere* is an American coinage from the French word for a bodice; in France, bras are called *soutien-gorges* (throat supporters).

● **SOUPED-UP SILHOUETTE**
Grace Jones gives new meaning to "form-fitting" in a zipped-up rubberized mock corset with projecting breasts.

GRAND CANYON

Décolletage is a language of many accents. Perched prettily as two distinct half-moons (achieved in the Renaissance by a padded triangle designed to lift and separate) or pressed together to form that magic channel known as cleavage, breasts rise boldly above the bodice line or beckon the beholder downward. As a nesting place for a locket, or itself a locket for billets-doux, this tender crease (sometimes accented with a touch of makeup) draws the eye toward unplumbed depths.

But despite a century of use, women are still choosing bras that don't really do the

"The only place men want depth in a woman is in her décolletage."
—*Zsa Zsa Gabor*

job. According to Victoria's Secret, 80 percent of women are walking around in wrong-size bras.

KNOW YOUR ABC'S

To find your correct bra size, you should measure the circumference of your rib cage just below the bust, then add 5 (for example, a measurement of 27 means you're a size 32). Next, wearing a bra, measure the circumference at the fullest part of the bust. The difference between the two measurements equals your cup size. (If the difference is one inch, your cup is an A; if the difference is 2.5 inches, you're a B; 3 inches brings you to a C; and 4 inches a D cup.)

 ROYAL FLUSH
Swooping right
down to the nipple,
this sixteenth-
century neckline
barely contains the
sitter's regal
breasts.

**A LITTLE GOES A
LONG WAY** With
emphasis less on
size than on pillowy
roundness, décol-
letage can create
much ado about not
so much.

DARING DIVIDE
Like a runway to
heaven, this cleav-
age leaves plenty of
room for takeoff.

TWO BOMBSHELLS
Dolly and Madonna
are masters in the art
of cleavage. Pressed
together, their breasts
create enough friction
to set fans on fire.

The Shifting Silhouette: A Time Line

S trictly utilitarian, the first recorded breast supporters were bands of woolen cloth designed for female Greek athletes who, excluded from the Olympic games, competed in a 500-foot race called the

Heraea (for the goddess Hera, sister and consort of Zeus). Similar breast bands called *mamillare*, pictured here as they were worn in third-century Sicily, were fashioned from soft leather.

● UP AND AT 'EM! A statuette of the Minoan snake goddess (c. 1550 B.C.) from the isle of Crete gives new meaning to the term *low cut*. Tightly fitted bands below the breasts don't quite account for their lift and forward propulsion.

A.D. 1200 to 1400

The corset first appeared when European women, influenced by fashion reports from Crusaders returning from the Holy Land, traded in their loose tunics for a more curvaceous silhouette—and greater breast support. After experimenting with pouches sewn into their dresses, they hit upon the innovative front-lacing corset, originally worn on the outside for a look we now associate with "folk" costumes.

1500 to 1600

Over time, the corset became increasingly restrictive. By the sixteenth century, it was an elongated garment stiffened by a "busk"—a strip of wood, horn, metal or whalebone inserted down the front from the bust to the hips. This vertical insert gained fame as an object of erotic interest, engraved with amorous verses and extolled in boudoir poetry.

 ELIZABETH I chose rigid corseting that minimized her femininity while enhancing her authority. In such tight girdling, she must indeed have walked with unbending majesty.

> "Unlace yourself, for that
> harmonious chime
> Tells me from you that it is now
> bed time.
> Off with that happy busk,
> which I envy,
> That still can be,
> and still can stand so nigh."

—John Donne, "To His Mistress Going to Bed"

1700s

The corset-flattened torso was rejected in favor of an inflated bosom, pushed up from below by means of wadding and whalebone, and sitting pretty above a low-cut bodice. (Sometimes even the nipples made an appearance.) As one contemporary humorist suggested, the breasts "which Nature planted at the bottom of her chest" were "perched to a station so near her chin that sometimes that feature is lost between the invading mounds."

Eighteenth-century engraving of corset, revealing nipples

In France, Napoleon sent corsets packing when it occurred to him that they interfered with pregnancy and thus with the birth of male heirs. Greek-inspired styles (along with the Greek ideal of democracy) enjoyed a vogue as women donned flimsy, one-piece muslin dresses over flesh-colored tights. Highlighting well-rounded breasts, including their often hidden underswelling, the Empire look was soon challenged and the corset, along with the monarchy, reseized control.

● FIGURES OF FUN
Until 1675, when the
French parliament first
allowed seamstresses
to make corsets, male
tailors monopolized
the industry and were
portrayed in caricatures,
ogling and prodding
their affluent clients'
ample bosoms.

THE GREAT CORSET CONTROVERSY

Corsets (and the exposure of the bosom) attracted controversy from early on. Medieval churchmen viewed the front lacings of bodices as "the gates of hell," and French essayist Montaigne attacked the corset as a torture device that women endured "even until they die of it." Nineteenth-century feminists compared wearing corsets to Chinese foot-binding and tried to legislate their extinction by proposing a corset tax.

Corsets and their bridled sweets accrued a host of contradictory connotations, from women's oppressed status, feminine vanity and womanly respectability to scandal, cheapness and the unchaste pleasures of tight-laced constraint giving way to illicit release. Less ambiguously, today's corsets function as occasional flourishes in haute couture or as objects of sexual play—Victoria's little secrets.

H. de Toulouse-Lautrec,
Passing Conquest, 1897

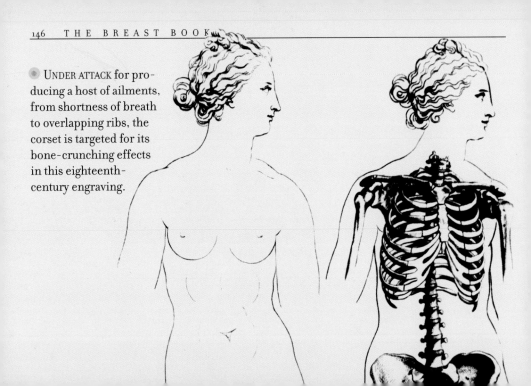

UNDER ATTACK for producing a host of ailments, from shortness of breath to overlapping ribs, the corset is targeted for its bone-crunching effects in this eighteenth-century engraving.

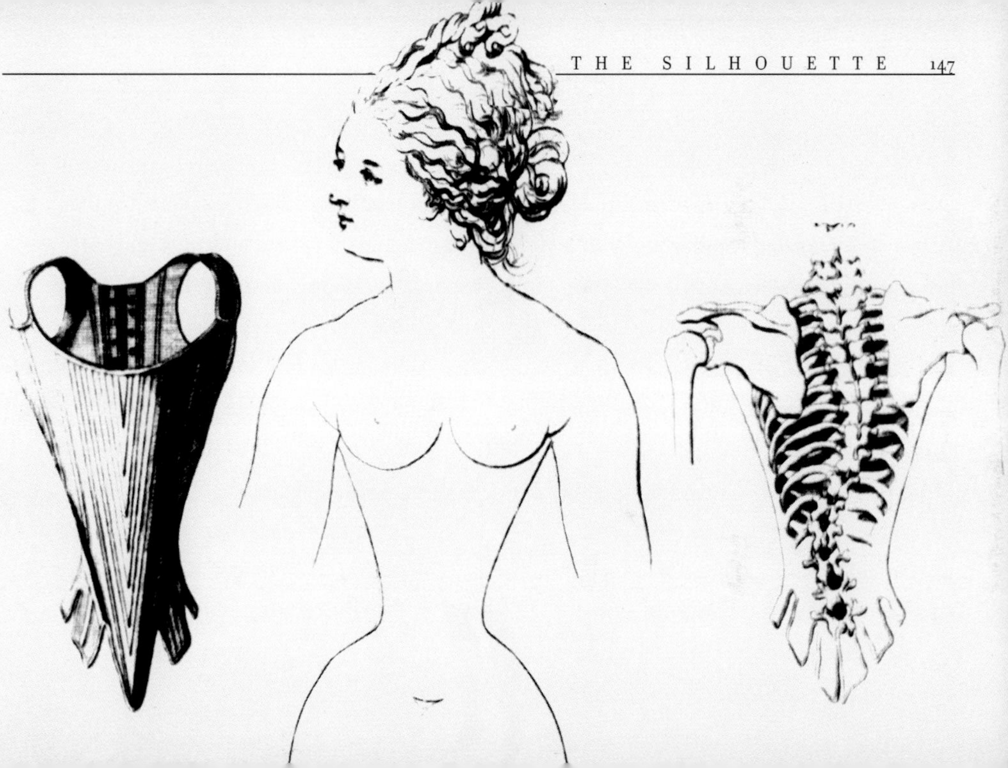

1800s

Corsetry reached lunatic extremes as women layered themselves with up to ten pounds of underwear. In 1823 the first mechanical corset was exhibited at the Exposition Universelle in Paris. Equipped with small pulleys, it allowed women to lace and unlace unassisted. With industrialization, machine-made corsets proliferated in models for all ages, conditions and occasions, including nursing, bathing and bicycling.

Beginning in the 1830s, as advertisements swelled fashion magazines, corsets appeared in artful shopwindow arrangements—naughty spectacles that found their way into etchings and early photographs. Widely displayed, these "unmentionables" blurred the line between function and seduction, female contraption and erotic fetish.

In 1885, "bust distenders," the first falsies, were introduced at London's Labor Exposition; they were placed inside corsets and inflated to the desired dimensions.

Right, Paris corset shop, c. 1900

Early 1900s

French couturier Paul Poiret broke with turn-of-the-century trends that distorted and constrained the female form to design women's apparel that followed and flattered a woman's natural shape. To Poiret it was unthinkable for breasts to be "sealed up in solitary confinement in a castle-like fortress . . . as if to punish them."

Although patents for designs that provided support from above rather than below had been granted as early as 1859, American debutante Mary Phelps Jacobs is generally credited with the invention of the brassiere.

Advertisement, c. 1910, predates the term brassiere.

In 1914, while dressing for a dance, she enlisted her French maid to help her sew two handkerchiefs together and attach pink ribbon for straps. The design caught fire in her social set and beyond, until one day she received a dollar in the mail from a woman requesting one. She soon patented her invention, dubbing it "the Backless Brassiere," and sold the patent to Warner Brothers Corset Company for $1,500; the patent was later valued at $15 million.

1914

Fashion called for "bust."

1915

*Pretty and sensible, but no uplift
or division.*

1923

*Fashion banished "bust."
Waistlines were large.*

● THE CORSET—A CASUALTY OF WAR

World War I helped derigidify the corset as American women pitched in to assist in arming the nation. Not only were metal-boned corsets banned from munitions factories, but a call from the War Industries Board urging women to stop buying steel-boned corsets diverted 28,000 tons of metal from the bosom to the battleship.

1916
*Woman in armament factory
with breasts unbound.*

1920s

W hen the flapper roared on to the scene, booze was not the only target of prohibition. Almost eradicating the breast, an elasticized bandeau-style bra helped women achieve the boyish flat look that was all the rage. After years of self-consciousness, they could appear (and perhaps feel) breast-free.

● THE SPORTY LOOK   The rise in the 1920s of women's sportswear, here worn by a youthful Joan Crawford, played its part in glamorizing the minimized bustline.

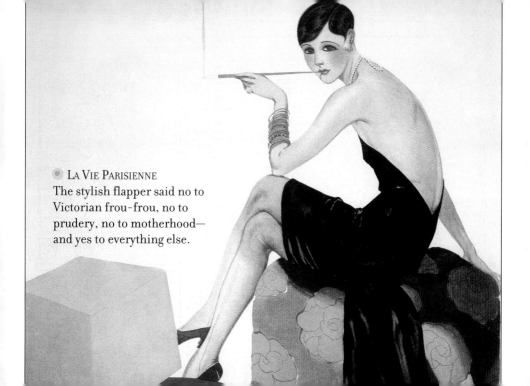

LA VIE PARISIENNE
The stylish flapper said no to
Victorian frou-frou, no to
prudery, no to motherhood—
and yes to everything else.

1930s to 1940s

Brassieres graduated to greater functionality, taking up the load for women of every shape and size. (Studies show that for bra purposes, there are five basic types of breasts.) Standardization of cup size was the brainchild of Maidenform founder Ida Rosenthal, but Warner's was the first to assign letters (A, B, C, D) that earned girls a second (peer-noted) report card.

"Brassiere" was abbreviated to "bra," and the first underwire number hit the market in 1938. Spiked and cantilevered over the waist, the new bra technology arrived just in time—to support the new full-bosom look, and to keep up the spirits of World War II servicemen. (As part of its war effort, Maidenform produced vests for carrier pigeons. In another connection between breasts and war, GIs called their life jackets "Mae Wests.")

Left, 1940 Varga Girl wearing an imaginary bra

● CODE BREAKERS   Howard Hughes, then America's wealthiest man, directed his aeronautics firm to design a no-bounce bra for girlfriend Jane Russell, constructed on the "suspension principle" and using calipers to measure depth and circumference, and calculating points of greatest stress. Most of this effort was meant to buck the Hollywood censorship code, which judged Russell's breasts in need of restraint. (Gossip columnist Walter Winchell's term for breasts was "janerussells.")

I dreamed
I took the bull
by the horns...
in my
*maidenform bra

1950s

Lingerie companies cottoned on to the idea that bras were not just a choice of quality or convenience but of identity. Couturiers began mass-producing bras, and lower-end marketers explored new advertising hooks. Maidenform's famous "I dreamed . . ." ad campaign took off and ran successfully for twenty years, reversing the familiar dream of appearing underdressed (and vulnerably exposed) in public so that expo-

THE LOVABLE GIRL-OF-THE-MONTH

ONLY $1⁵⁰

Bull's-eye: Circular stitching makes this bra "lovable."

sure became empowering and subtly erotic.

"Perfect" bust-waist-hip measurements (34-24-36) became shorthand for "sexy." Breasts headlined a curvy but distinctly angular silhouette—bold and well contained. Everybody wanted to get into the act, and bra makers expanded their trade with a complete line of lingerie for teenagers and training bras for preteens.

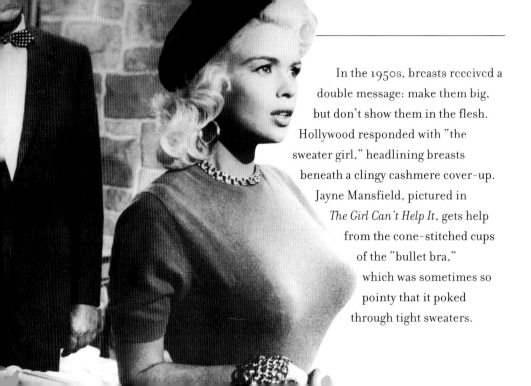

In the 1950s, breasts received a double message: make them big, but don't show them in the flesh. Hollywood responded with "the sweater girl," headlining breasts beneath a clingy cashmere cover-up. Jayne Mansfield, pictured in *The Girl Can't Help It*, gets help from the cone-stitched cups of the "bullet bra," which was sometimes so pointy that it poked through tight sweaters.

THE MERRY WIDOW, a strapless corset, was part of a trend of labeling undergarments with names like Pink Champagne and Charade; using the demi-cup (a bra cup cut in half to leave the upper part of the bosom exposed), this number was marketed with an ad campaign that asked: "How can you look so naughty and feel so nice?" Brigitte Bardot answers the question, *en français*.

1960s

The bra industry responded scattershot to bra-burning feminists and sixties mods with the "no-bra bra," the stretch bra and bras in psychedelic colors and patterns. Still, many opted to do without.

"Free as the dawn in the new life, sister," reads this bra ad from Berlei.

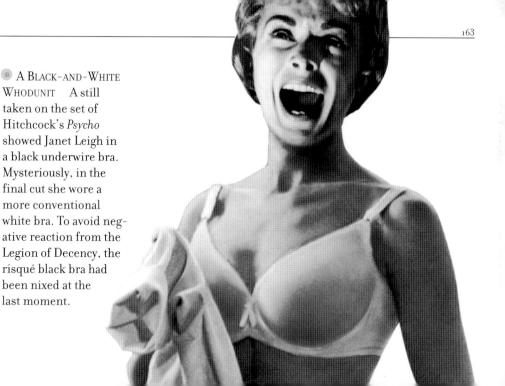

A BLACK-AND-WHITE
WHODUNIT   A still
taken on the set of
Hitchcock's *Psycho*
showed Janet Leigh in
a black underwire bra.
Mysteriously, in the
final cut she wore a
more conventional
white bra. To avoid neg-
ative reaction from the
Legion of Decency, the
risqué black bra had
been nixed at the
last moment.

1970s and 1980s

"Motion control" was the challenge of the day as women took to the fitness trail. Confronting the problem of the bounce, two female jogging enthusiasts

stitched together a pair of jockstraps to produce the first jogging bra—and sports bras were off and running.

● "BraBall," a five-foot-four-inch sphere constructed of 7,000 bras was artist Emily Duffy's protest against "the way breasts have been overly emphasized." Women from all over the world offered their support by donating their bras.

● On a rainy day in 1986, a Buddhist priest blessed 200,000 cast-off brassieres, arranged in a pyramid, at a memorial service in Tokyo.

1990s

The Wonderbra, with its double-click system (two clicks for more cleavage), hit the American market with literal fanfare: the first shipment arrived at Macy's in New York in a cable car full of cheerleaders and was greeted by opera tenors singing the bra's praises to crowds of eager shoppers.

As an intimate contribution to the Japanese new year festivities, a lingerie manufacturer constructed a "millennial bra" made of solid gold. Retail price: $1.9 million.

2000

Bra technology's latest breakthrough is the Bioform Bra. Touted as a rethinking of the fundamentals of bra design that

will antiquate the underwire bra, it draws on expertise from the automotive and construction industries. The molded cups are cantilevered to push breasts up from the sides, thus relieving shoulder pain.

A bra for the twenty-first century

SECOND BASE

Over the years, whether fussing with elaborate corset lacing or fretting with bra hooks in the backseat, sexual partners have been receiving signals from undergarments. Servicing modesty or eros—or a compromise between the two—these anatomical accessories have constituted the last line of sexual resistance, in PC terms, both yes and no.

Now that undergarments have emerged from the bedroom, fashion sends these mixed signals out onto the street—though in the white noise of sexual suggestion, we now know that until she unhooks her bra

herself, everything means no. As fashion accessories, bras have emerged from the bedroom. An exposed bra strap once suggested sexual license; now it declares sexual pride.

FASHION VICTIMS EVERYWHERE swooned when Madonna collaborated with Jean Paul Gaultier on a costume for her 1994 world tour. Mixing a corset with cone-shaped breasts, inspired by the New Look, the Material Girl further erased the line between underwear and outerwear.

GETTING THEM RIGHT

"Breasts come in two sizes: too big or too small."
—Joanie Blank

Not too long ago, vanity was considered one of the deadly sins. Aspiring to improve your looks rather than your virtue was thought to be morally degrading, and most beauty alterations (like taking arsenic to improve your complexion) were performed sub rosa. Today, however, women claim the right to perfect their bodies, or, as they say in twelve-step programs, to change what they have the power to change. "Be all you can be" has become the modern woman's mantra—and she's free to use whatever tools are at hand.

Previous page, Jeanette MacDonald in Love Me Tonight, *1932; right, a drawing from a 1921 magazine shows women concerned that they won't fit in with the decade's flat-chested look.*

THE SCIENCE OF PERFECTION

Since the dawn of time, women have looked for secret ways to change their breasts, hoping to trick nature at her own game. Sold door-to-door by quacks or concocted by early medics, lotions, tonics, creams and pills have all promised a bigger bustline, or, as the advertisements say, usually in capital letters, to "INCREASE BREAST SIZE—GUARANTEED!" Historic examples include recipes from members of the French court: in the late fifteenth century, Eleanor (favored mistress of Charles VII) preserved her bosom with regular doses of poppy water, a mixture of ivy, rose oil and camphor; Diane de Poitiers was rumored to wash her celebrated breasts in a compound of gold and rainwater or sow's milk. By the end of the nineteenth century, purveyors used the new forms of technology and advertising to present a host of options. An 1897 Sears, Roebuck catalog offered solutions to those women "whom nature has not favored." Hope came in the form of a "Princess Bust Developer" (a device resembling a

90°

The perfect breast is a matter of degree in this ideal formula.

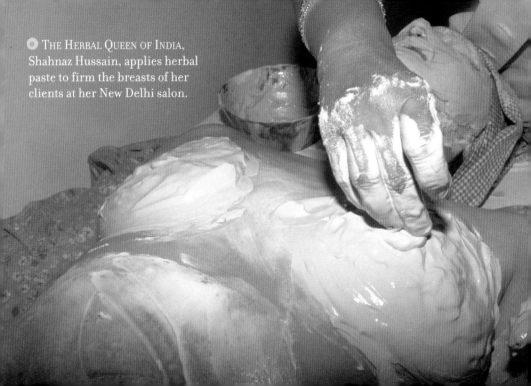

THE HERBAL QUEEN OF INDIA, Shahnaz Hussain, applies herbal paste to firm the breasts of her clients at her New Delhi salon.

plunger) and miracle salves like Seroco Chemical Laboratories' "Bust Cream," a substance "unrivalled for enlargement."

Ultimately, as doctors' goals came to include aesthetic ideals, cosmetic surgeries became not just legitimate but standard practice and plastic surgeons, once considered quacks, are now social darlings with triple-loaded degrees. In the year 2000, more than 1.3 million Americans had plastic surgery, a rise of 198 percent since 1992. And over the last decade women looking for more "womanly" figures have reached record proportions.

Cosmetic alteration can also beg some very difficult questions. Surgery is an option, if you want to say less, say more, or just say something different. If your aim is to downsize, upgrade or reverse

● FIRST LADY OF IMPLANTS
Dolly Parton, a veritable icon of self-actualization, flew in the face of fashion and created a style all her own. Good-natured Dolly has said of her breasts: "I don't know if I'm supporting them or they're supporting me, but they've served me well. I love being girlie, and I love my boobs."

"We must, we must,
we must increase our bust,
the bigger the better,
the tighter the sweater,
the boys are counting on us!"

—popular girls chant
from the '40s

A plethora of nineteenth-century breast "improving" products promised to make any woman a real doll.

aging, according to this logic, there is a breast out there that says YOU. And when Wonderbra advertises with the tag line "When I look good, I feel good and when I feel good, I look great," they are expressing the idea that changing your bustline can change your life. But as physical ideals boomerang over time, there can be trouling aspects to the long-term effects of the surgeon's knife on a woman's self-perception. Even the American Society for Plastic Surgeons cautions that cosmetic surgery is a very "personal question" and that the best candidates for it should be looking for "improvement, not perfection."

● DIMINISHING RETURNS   Pamela Anderson
Lee, the bodacious former star of TV's
Baywatch, has literally become synonymous
with her breasts. Whether bouncing beach-
side or hitting the nightspots, she wore
her outsized implants like life vests in the
stormy waters of her romantic life. When
she decided to downsize to "just a handful,"
her career took a nosedive.

*"When we consider the significant
cultural shifts of the past few years,
the removal of Pamela Anderson's
breast implants must rank
right up there at the top."*
—Suzanne Moore

IS BIGGER REALLY BETTER?

> *"Size is destiny."*
> —*Mim Udovitch*

Breast enlargement, from its inception, was pumped up by its share of inflammatory rhetoric. Larger breasts, doctors in the first half of the twentieth century promised, would free women from "the bondage of inferiority" or solve the problem of "hypomastia," a term invented by doctors to describe the "medical condition" of small or undersized breasts and related feelings of inadequate femininity, shyness, social and sexual withdrawal and depression.

Don't bel

what the

Size mat

ve

ay.

rs.

RIA BRAVA

Plastic surgery is extremely popular in Latin America, where teenage girls often receive cosmetic operations as "sweet fifteen" presents. But different operations are popular in different regions. Brazil, home of the string bikini, favors breast reductions, while Argentina prefers breast implants: over one million breast enlargement operations have been performed there since 1970, about one for every thirty women.

An X ray of a breast with a silicone implant

Early attempts to enlarge breasts, including the injection of goats' milk, paraffin and fat from other areas of the body, proved long-term failures.

Today, breast augmentation is the second most popular surgical procedure in the United States. Since 1992, the year of the silicone controversy, the number of patients has increased by 476 percent and in 2000 alone 187,755 operations were performed. (In 1999, more than 1,800 American girls under the age of eighteen had breast implants with the consent of their parents; most of these surgeries were performed in California, Florida and Texas.) At a cost averaging between $4,000 and $5,000, this is not cheap chic. Nor is it small change: surgical augmentation promises an increase of one full cup size at the bare minimum.

CAROL DODA became a living monument to silicone injections when, in the early 1960s, she put herself on display at the first modern topless bar in San Francisco's North Beach. Loyal customers could monitor her weekly growth rate, as her breasts ballooned from a 34D to 44DD.

1st MAW

TO
MISS CAROL DODA
OUR
"GIRL MOST DESIRABLE"

WE THE MEN OF THE 1st MARINE AIRCRAFT
WING ADJUTANT SECTION DO HEREBY
BESTOW UPON YOU THIS TITLE WITH
CONTINUED BEST WISHES AND SUCCESS.

Best Always,
Carol Doda

DOES SHE OR DOESN'T SHE? Only her plastic surgeon knows for sure .

Melanie Griffith

Mariah Carey

Tori Spelling

L'il Kim

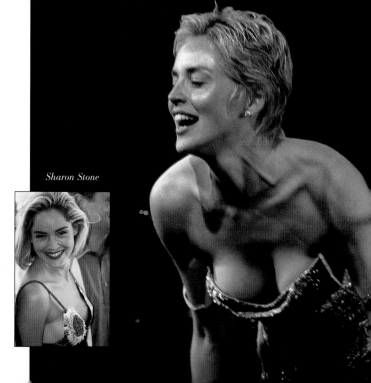

"Tits and ass
can change your life,
they sure changed mine.
Have it all done.
Honey, take my word.
Grab a cab, c'mon,
See the wizard on Park
and Seventy-third
For Tits and Ass.
Orchestra and balcony."
—A Chorus Line

Sharon Stone

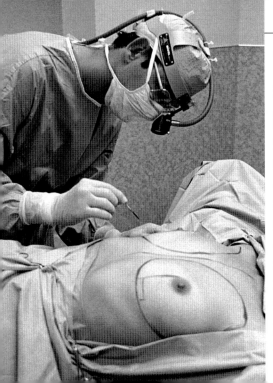

THE SILICONE STORY

Successful breast augmentation began with the development of the liquid polymer silicone in 1943 as part of the war effort. Though most accounts locate the first use of liquid silicone for breast enlargement in wartime Japan, where cosmetologists injected it into prostitutes, the first implanting of silicone gel (liquid silicone in a hard silicone capsule) was performed by Texas plastic surgeons Thomas D. Cronin and Frank J. Gerow in 1963. Their surgical method of inserting silicone pouches through a side incision, either in front of the gland or behind the muscle wall, has remained the standard procedure for breast enlargement.

Reports of implant-related diseases and conditions, such as cancer and arthritis, caused by ruptures allowing silicone to enter the bloodstream, persuaded the FDA to stipulate that the use of silicone should be limited until further research had proven it safe. Though civil damages were awarded to claimants against Dow Corning for injuries attributed to silicone breast implants, recent research has found no direct correlation between silicone and illness, and on May 10, 2000, the FDA approved silicone-filled implants for further research purposes.

The majority of implants used in the last ten years have been saline-filled with silicone gel casings. This, however, has not eliminated problems. Though breast augmentation surgery has now been widely performed for nearly fifty years, practice has not made perfect, and nearly half the implant removals in the United States in the year 2000 (around 16,000) were due to capsular contracture,

Saline (top) and silicone implants

where the capsule around the implant tightens, making the implant hard and the skin dimpled; nearly a third were due to the rupturing of the capsule itself. There is also the risk of infection, calcium deposits and the loss of nipple or breast sensation. Still, nearly 89 percent of the women whose implants were removed had them replaced— and many will have them replaced again. As the surgery literature reads (if only in the fine print), these new breasts—like all breasts, which change over time—are only *semi*permanent.

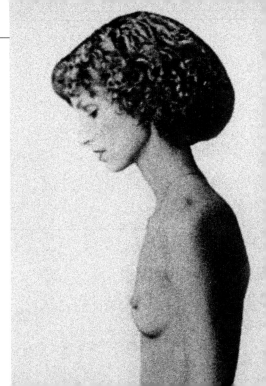

⬤ FULL SUPPORT   In 1970, the same year that Dow Corning estimated it had sold 50,000 implants in the first seven years of their manufacture, *Cosmopolitan* published its own finding that "surgically augmented breasts have a better contour than the real thing. They stand up . . . will not sag or droop or get flaccid. They're firm and solid."

Dr. JACK SAYS...
I NEVER PLANNED FOR MY WORK TO GET AS BIG AS IT IS!

MAKE SURE
YOU'RE SAFE
from
TB
Check YOUR CHEST
GET YOUR Free
X-RAY TODAY
IN GREATER CLEVELAND'S COMMUNITY-WIDE SURVEY

**City Males Puff Out Chests;
Females Have Few 'Falsies'**

BY ROELIF LOVELAND

THE TRUTH ABOUT FALSIES

Stuffing for effect may have even occurred among cavewomen (rocks in your bearskin), but supplements specifically designed to plump up the breasts' natural shape is a more recent development. Not until the nineteenth century did manufacturers take the hint and begin offering ready-made means of temporary breast enhancement. Early devices ranged from cup-shaped wires on flexible celluloid to vests with circular pockets for an insertable wool pad (wool itched but didn't lump like cotton). Later designers and inventors toyed with differ-ent materials: synthetic rubber was used to make breast pads, dubbed "lemon bosoms" for their shape and size. In the 1870s, Frederick Cox came up with breast pads that were inflated like balloons. And attempts to simulate the breasts' natural feel and weight by filling plastic pouches with water or oil came and went—probably with some embarrassing moments—in the 1930s. By the 1950s, inventors were apply-ing the blow-up concept to new durable plastics with the added advantage of hand-held pumps. Since these new models were given to leaking (and, on poorly pressurized airplanes, exploding), multicompartmental bladders were invented in an attempt to solve sudden, dispiriting deflation.

The heyday of falsies came in the fifties—a time when, as J. D. Salinger wrote in *The Catcher in the Rye*, everyone wore "those damn falsies that point all over the place."

● THE INVENTION OF SILICONE revolutionized falsies, too. The silicone pouches called Curves™ were launched in 1995 as "Hollywood's Best Kept Secret" —for starlets or fans who want to plump up at will. Designed to be slipped into a bra, they are also known as "chicks" because they look like chicken breasts.

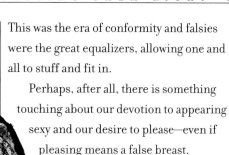

This was the era of conformity and falsies were the great equalizers, allowing one and all to stuff and fit in.

Perhaps, after all, there is something touching about our devotion to appearing sexy and our desire to please—even if pleasing means a false breast.

Ironically, women pad their chests to attract attention with hopes of getting someone to want to see the real thing.

 STRAP-ONS   The "breast-pad harness," as depicted at the turn of the eighteenth century, was a precursor of the modern bra—complete with elastic straps for the best possible fit.

NIP AND TUCK

Perhaps this is the untold story of breasts: if they're too large, they can be both uncomfortable and unwanted. Macromastia can also be physically debilitating and can cause neck, shoulder, back and breast pain, headaches, numbness and rashes, as well as grooves from bra straps. Many prospective breast reduction patients also report difficulty with exercise. (For these reasons, breast reduction is still considered a reconstructive rather than a cosmetic operation.) In addition, many women with large breasts receive undesired sexual attention. Unlike women who choose to have large breasts, they may not be interested in displaying theirs and may in fact dislike having their sexuality announced for them in a kind of pre-parade salute.

Reduction mammaplasty, or breast reduction, attracts about half the number of women who want augmentation and is usually a more expensive operation, costing about $8,000. Moreover, recovery time is longer and the patient is left with more visible scar tissue. But studies show that women who receive breast reductions have a much higher rate of long-term satisfaction. In fact, one study showed that 84 percent

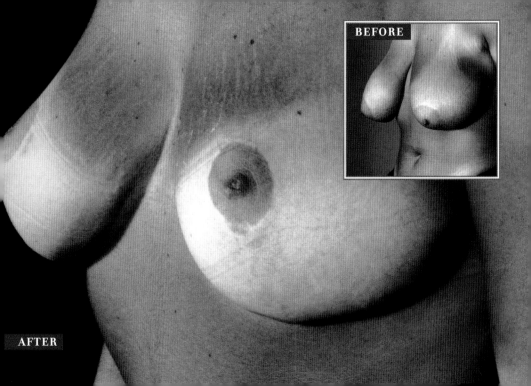

BEFORE

AFTER

were very satisfied, and 95 percent said they would recommend it to other women.

The earliest breast operations were actually reductions: reconstructive solutions for the physical side effects of macromastia, diseases or cancerous growths. Problems of excessive breast size are first referred to by Paulus of Aegina in the sixth century. Early operations, of which there are few accounts, were mostly fatal. The first full report of a breast reduction dates to 1893; after performing a partial mastectomy to remove a growth, the surgeon economically harvested fat from a "fortunate" (noncancerous)

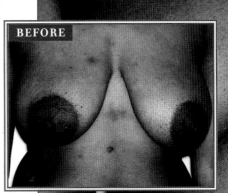

BEFORE

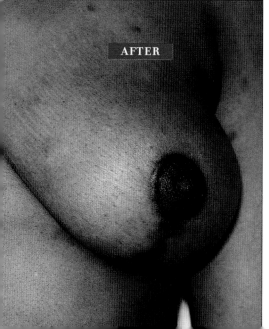

AFTER

The LeJour method makes a lollipop (rather than a horseshoe) scar.

lipoma on the patient's back and attempted to reshape the surviving breast. Later surgical developments minimized scarring and moved the nipple to a new, more "normal" position.

The type of operation generally performed today dates to the 1920s. The mammary gland is removed from the lower half of the breast, the nipple is removed and repositioned, and the result is an anchor-shaped scar that circles below the new (smaller) breast with a line running down from the nipple. Possible side effects include the loss of nipple sensation and the ability to breast-feed. (Patients with extremely large breasts may have already suffered from both these ailments.) Some surgeons now advocate the LeJour method, an outpatient surgery that cuts a figure eight around the areola; the skin flaps are used to move the areola up and secure it to the chest wall.

Breast lifts, otherwise known as masto-pexys, use the same surgical method as breast reductions without removing the breast tissue. This procedure is gaining popularity among mature women, who don't want different breasts, just the reversal of time, back to the days when their breasts still turned up.

FAST FORWARD

Bigger, smaller, higher, lower—we still don't always know quite who has done what. Maybe "realness" isn't the point and maybe the future will look less and less like the past. Ultra-femininity (ultra-large breasts, hips, lips) might become the new ideal: recent scientific evidence may support the claim that the breast-tissue enhancer called the Brava Bra, a suction-cup device run by a computer microchip, stimulates cell growth. Maybe we'll go ultra-masculine (chin, ab, pec implants), or have a body constructed of entirely new parts.

Or maybe we'll just look more like ourselves: research on cloning has revealed that it is possible to grow nipples and associated mammary gland tissue from human cartilage cells. And some tissue engineers predict that whole breasts will be ready for transplant (back to their owners?) by the year 2006.

"A Modern Venus,"
1786 engraving

THE JEWEL IN THE CROWN

". . . nipple flat as a stroke of color
a spot where some god had laid a thumb
for an instant . . ."
—Sharon Olds, "For My Mother"

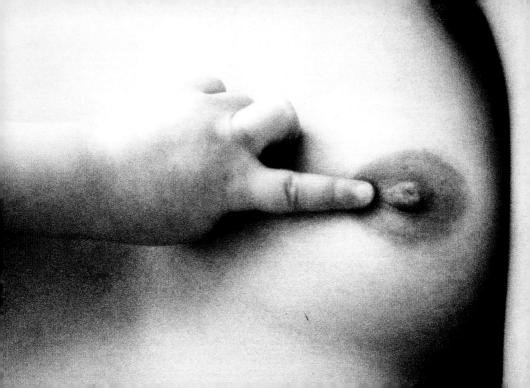

Principal players in the breast's organizing aesthetic, nipples call out for the eye's attention. The German word for nipple is *Brustwarze*, literally translated as "breast wart," but the center of the breast is not just an addendum or accidental growth. In their functional mode, nipples are first and foremost the exit points for milk—the nozzles on the breast machine. Without them, the breasts would be just another fatty area like the buttocks: friendly, squeezable, but lacking the ability to sustain life and the point—of pleasure.

Marcel Duchamp,
Priere de Toucher,
1947

MAGIC CIRCLE

Around within a round, the nipple is both an adornment to the breast and its finishing flourish—a lipstick kiss. For really it's the nipple *on* the breast that's the site of erotic interest. If nipples are at the heart of breast fixation—often standing in for breasts themselves—maybe it's because nipples are what make breasts beautiful. The evolution of the word *tit* hints at the conflation between breast and nipple. In its original Anglo-Saxon usage, *tit* referred only to the nipple. (The whole breast was called an *uder*, an earlier form of *udder*, and a word that smacks of function over form.) When the Normans invaded England, they converted the vulgar *tit* to *teat*, still commonly used for the nonhuman mammalian nipple. But *tit* stayed in the language as the word for a delicate morsel, or "tit bit," and in the Roaring Twenties its slang meaning broadened to cover the entire breast.

TITTY TWEAKING   Perhaps the most famous image involving nipples—or at least where nipples are being played with to the edge of pain—is this portrait of Henry IV's mistress, Gabrielle d'Estrées, and her sister in the bath. In today's school yards, the more vicious version of this game is called titty twister.

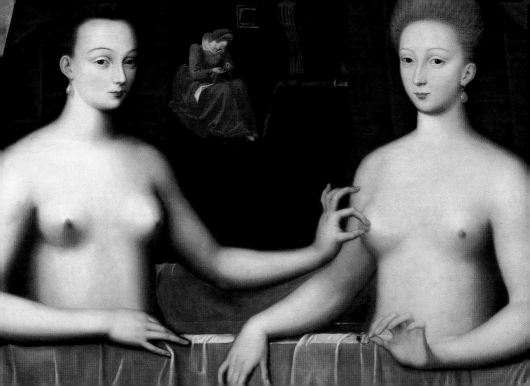

Tweaked, these nipples show their reaction.

TENDER BUTTONS

Like everything else divinely human, nipples express our stubborn individuality by exhibiting a tremendous variation in shape, size and coloring. They can be round, elliptical or cylindrical in shape, and their areolae—the surrounding pigmented region—can be small and tidy or large and blurry. They also differ in profile, showing themselves puffed out, snubbed or even inverted, and come in a range of colors and hues from dun to rosy red to burgundy, depending on the thinness and pigmentation of the skin.

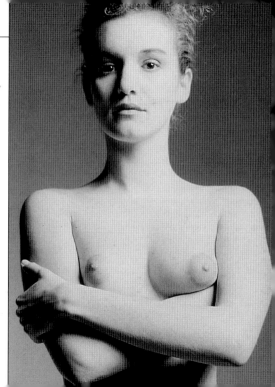

Home to a concentration of nerve end-ings, nipples can be extremely sensitive to touch and cold and even inner feelings, although they differ in levels of respon-siveness. Special muscle fibers running through the nipple and areola respond to stimulation and cause erection. Some peo-ple's nipples stiffen at the slightest brush—or just a hint of romance in the air, while others need a more vigorous approach. (Like earlobes, not everyone likes theirs chewed!) Some are even constantly erect, twin signals that may indicate neither a wintry chill nor a state of perpetual arousal.

● HOT SPOTS
If burning cigarette embers are often called cherries, everyone feels the heat—and the promise of pleasure.

"yes I think he made them a bit firmer
sucking them like that so long he
made me thirsty titties he calls them
I had to laugh yes this one anyhow
stiff the nipple gets for the least thing"

—James Joyce, Ulysses

Right, Egon Schiele,
Kneeling Semi-Nude, *1917*

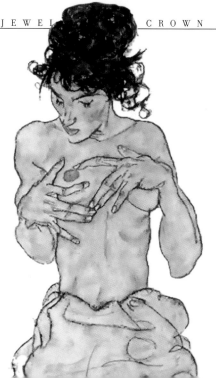

During pregnancy the nipples' areolae darken and swell as if to announce a shift in emphasis from form to function. In this portrait by Alice Neel, her friend Margaret Evans's nipples are like huge shadows almost obscuring her breasts.

After one gives birth, the nipple secretes oil from tiny raised bumps, which lubricates and protects the nipple from the wear and tear of suckling.

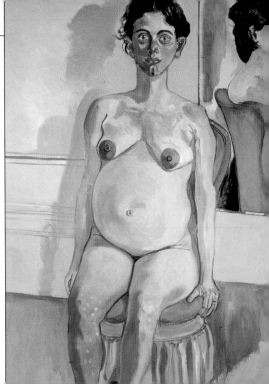

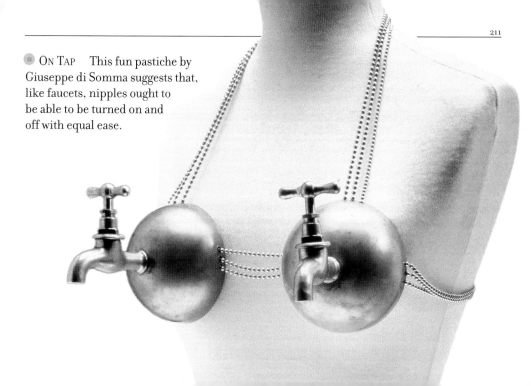

ON TAP This fun pastiche by Giuseppe di Somma suggests that, like faucets, nipples ought to be able to be turned on and off with equal ease.

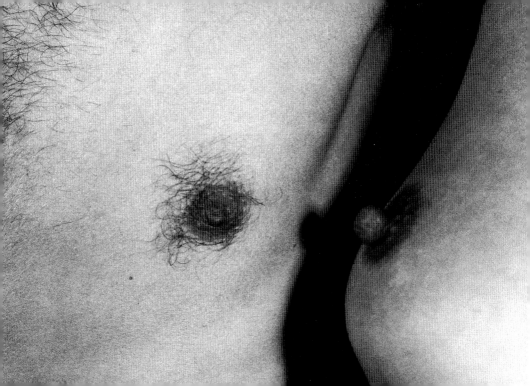

● HIS AND HERS   Male nipples don't get much fanfare, but they have feelings, too. Darwin theorized that the reason men (and most male mammals) have nipples is that both sexes yielded milk in our species' early stages.

● DUELING NIPPLES   As if vying for superior erotic charge, these nipples appear to be puffing up to challenge each other. Nipples can quicken at the blink of an eye and deflate just as quickly, stiffening and softening like a flower under the watchful gaze of a high-speed camera.

FIT FOR A FEAST

We receive our first feasts from nursing, so it makes sense that we see nipples as sweet foods—and that cherries atop sundaes will always have an irresistible, cheerily erotic appeal. Fruity desserts have been favorite analogies for artists who wanted to portray nipples as precious treats. Like berry stains after a fruitful picnic, Modigliani's nipples recall the residue of a satisfying meal. And as far back as the fifteenth century, Raphael painted colorless nipples, barely there, that hinted at subtler pleasures.

Facing page, from left: Modigliani, Nu Assis, Au Collier; Lorenzi, little Parisian sparrow; Raphael, La Fornarina

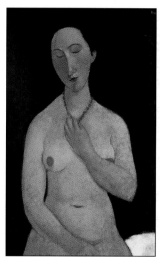  

"... taste the ripened Cherry, / The warme, firme Apple, / tipt with corall berry"
—Thomas Carew, "A Rapture"

OPALS CAPPED WITH RUBIES,
these breasts shine like
strangely swollen jewels.
Or as Randy Newman sings:
"And that little blue vein
right beneath her breast
Man those nipples
Pink as a rosebud!"

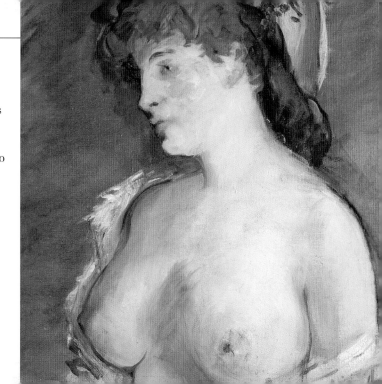

SWEETNESS AND LIGHT
Manet and other Impressionists painted blurry, generous nipples that seem to have been dabbed in a soft, custardy substance—ready to be licked clean.

Right Back at You

Paired with the eyes of their owner, nipples can literally double the power of a straightforward challenge or an erotic stare, fixing us with the measure of their gaze. In other cases, they can seem as pert and irrepressible as a coquettish wink. Some artists have used the nipple as a kind of organizing principle, a point of pause or a literal eye in the storm, creating a vortex of feeling in the beholder.

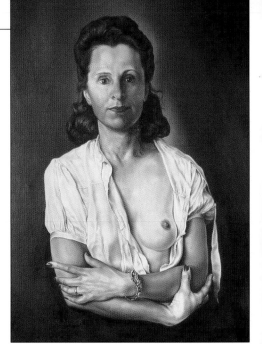

"Nipples in still pictures
are as varied and
communicative
as women's eyes. . . ."
—Nicholson Baker

Far left, Salvador Dali,
Gala; *left, Lucian Freud,*
Girl with a White Dog

DON'T LOOK! Nipples can also serve as foils for the modesty of their owners. In these early erotic photographs, the nipple is soft and demure, turning a blind eye to the naughtiness at hand.

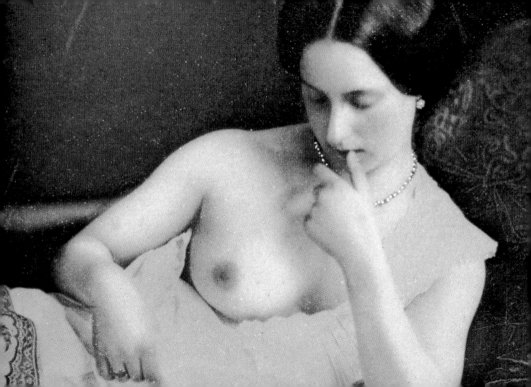

KEEPING AN EYE OUT, these long-limbed bodies are wrapped around themselves in temporary rest, waiting to see what the next moment will bring. Sleep may be imminent, but the erotic eye is ever watchful.

Right, Lee Friedlander, nude, 1978; far right, Gustav Klimt, Danae

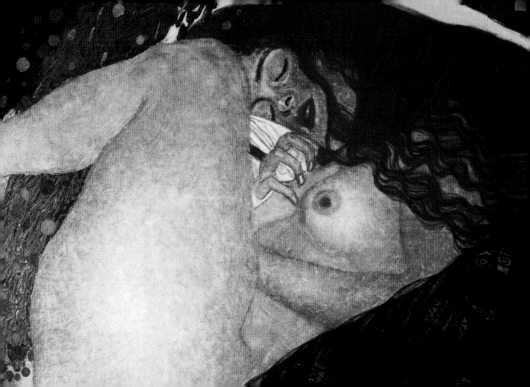

Put-Ons

At certain points in modern history, nipple exposure was all the rage. In late-eighteenth-century France, for example, nipples came up for air as bodice lines in fashionable circles dropped, giving a whole new meaning to "breathing room." But even though they're regularly featured in haute couture runway shows, exposed nipples have rarely entered street fashion.

Nipples are the chief culprit in modern America's skeptical view toward women who bare their breasts in public. Most nudity legislation stipulates that the nipple

Far left, French fashions c. 1775; left, Sharon Harlow in a 1999 fashion show

and areola be covered, and pasties, in those states that require them, must cover only the nipple itself. Band-Aids placed over nipples (sometimes even before breasts appear or in lieu of wearing a bra) are an early version of self-censorship, as when the Hollywood code added nipples to the no-no list. Nipples were not to be seen again in American movies until the 1960s.

Yet pasties sometimes have the opposite effect. Like the gold paint that women in ancient Egypt applied to their nipples, these cover-ups highlight the very features they were meant to hide.

Pasties move from striptease to French advertising.

BOSOM BUDDY The newest development in nipple technology is, perhaps not surprisingly, another silicone illusion. This time it's in the form of a nipple-shaped stick-on designed to be inserted into a bra—or worn just on its own "for flirty fun." The result is a set of nipples that look perpetually swollen, permanently hard, always excited and perfect for (advertisements declare) "a night on the town" or "a game of volleyball"!

STUCK ON YOU

Nipple piercing, for its advocates, can accentuate the pleasure-pain dynamic—the sweet bite—although it sets some teeth on edge. Whether for ornamental effect or to enhance sexual pleasure for yourself or a partner, unlike more common and public piercings (like earlobes), nipple piercing is largely for private viewing.

It's not clear when nipple piercing was first practiced in Western cultures. Some authorities suggest that Roman soldiers kept their capes in place with nipple rings. Queen Isabella of Bavaria, wife of the mad Charles VI

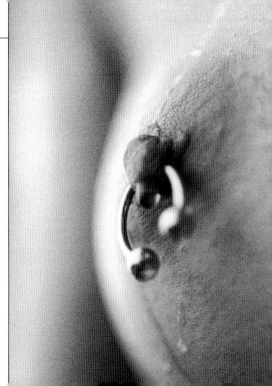

of France, is credited with starting a fashion in the fifteenth century for "garments of the grand neckline"; as these low-cut dresses exposed at least half the breast, the court experimented with ways to highlight the nipple's ornamental properties, applying rouge and eventually devising piercings like diamond rings and caps threaded with small chains. Other lore includes the idea that nipple piercings were prescribed by physicians in Victorian London to rid women of inverted nipples. Some apocryphal evidence points to a small vogue, along with spiritualism and the raising of the dead, for pierced nipples as a sexual accessory in Edwardian London.

More recently, nipple piercing (along with piercing of other kinds) has served as a kind of physical or sexual rebellion. Whether you're a teenager (showing your parents that you don't share their staid sexual mores) or an adult (who wants to show you're not *that* old), nipple piercings can also be a declaration of Buyer Beware: don't touch if you can't take the heat.

LITTLE BARBELLS, buried in tender flesh, hint at the strength and toughness of their owner. They're kept almost hidden until the wearer opens her shirt to show what she's made of.

THE VEILED EROTIC

"Is not the most erotic space of the body where the clothing gapes?
. . . that part of the skin which glistens between two pieces . . ."
—Roland Barthes

What makes something sexy is almost impossible to define. True, the erotic charge usually begins with the breasts, and an eyeful makes a potent statement: "Look what I can do to you." But even more tantalizing is the hint of more to come. Perhaps that's why we veil or adorn our breasts as a kind of Coming Attraction, because nakedness—the exposed, unadorned body—is, well, not *as* sexy. Adorning the body heightens anticipation and transforms nakedness into eros. In concealing something that might be arousing to others, you up the ante on what's revealed.

● MUTUAL ATTRACTION
Even the smallest open-
ing activates what Freud
called the "libido for
looking," seduction
through the eye. Self-
display carries its own
autoerotic zing, focusing
and controlling erotic
interest even in the
mirror.

*Previous spread, School
of Fontainebleau,* Portrait
of a Woman;
left, Titian, Flora

RAISING THE ANTE

Women are masterful players in the high-stakes game of sexiness. By ornamenting herself or putting on a sexy outfit, a woman toys with the boundaries between power and its relinquishment; she's taking charge while exploring the perimeters of her own pleasure, not least at the sight of her own appeal.

● KICKING THE HABIT   When what is habitually covered up is laid bare, erotic attention focuses there. In this case, the nun reveals a breast worthy of adulation.

TOP BILLING Josephine Baker was the risqué sensation of the 1920s Paris stage—her outrageous costumes made her glitter with erotic can-do. As Jean Cocteau said upon seeing her: "eroticism has found a style."

PEEKABOO

Who, me? Sometimes clothing slips off, sometimes it's shrugged off—but whether or not it's intentional, a breast, like a surprise guest, most often finds a warm welcome. Peeping out from a body otherwise clothed, the breast is naked in a sea of dress, creating a climate of erotic abandon.

This is the eros of accident, where what's partially seen insists on the rest being imagined. What's there—a shy nipple, the dusky curve beneath—takes root in the fertile ground of imagination, with the promise of more to come. Is the clothing conspiring to

undress her or is she undressing herself? Is the breast (with its nipple eye)
looking at you? What's sexy here is the
ambiguous nature of the disarray—an
inherent conflict in the gesture and the
anxiety of interpretation.

● A GUESSING GAME   Is she pulling
her shirt on or shucking it off?
Moments like this, halfway in either
direction, convey the ambivalent effect
of the breast's appearance—in and out
of view.

"*A sweet disorder in the dress*
Kindles in clothes a wantonness."
—Robert Herrick

Left, Édouard Manet,
Jeune fille deshabille;
right, Natalie Schiavoni,
The Sleeper

THE MINOR SLIPPAGE that reveals this youthful, creamy breast may have been caused by a deep, sleepy sigh. Are her dreams perhaps sweetened by this passive exposure?

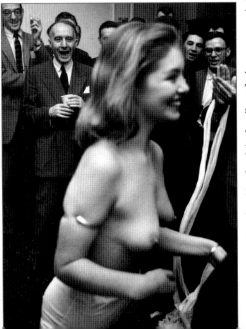

LESS IS MORE

Although we associate covering up with inhibition, modesty is on intimate terms with titillation. The act of trying to hide what might be stimulating to others can be extremely erotic. It's not exactly that the body or breasts au naturel aren't fetching, but the cult of the body (like all cults, where cloaking increases mystique) is sustained by secrecy—through a method of speech where insinuation speaks louder than a direct statement.

Left, Elliott Erwitt

● THE PARADOX OF MODESTY reached its height in the Victorian era, when a barely visible ankle or a hint of calf was endowed with all the allure of a highly charged erotic zone.

Left, J. Lindar,
Bathing Beauties, *1862;*
right, Robert Flynt,
Untitled, *1996*

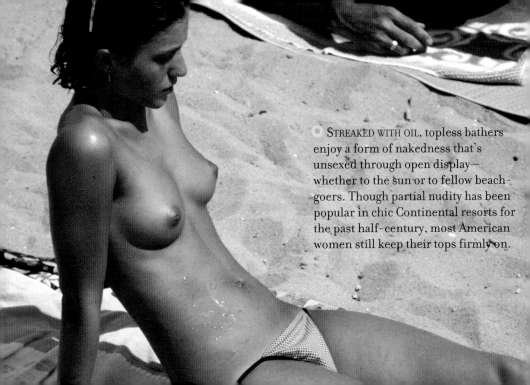

STREAKED WITH OIL, topless bathers enjoy a form of nakedness that's unsexed through open display—whether to the sun or to fellow beach-goers. Though partial nudity has been popular in chic Continental resorts for the past half-century, most American women still keep their tops firmly on.

 A WET T-SHIRT says it all without baring all and makes a strong case for how "less is more."

THE ART OF ADORNMENT

As writer Natalie Angier has noted, the breast itself—flamboyant, irresistible and decorative—is an adornment of the body. But even the smallest ornament can signal the difference between being bare and being available, between being unclothed and being undressed. It takes very little—a tiara, a tattoo, a polished fingernail—to transform the body

from a birthday suit to an erotic vista.

Adornment is an eroticizing gesture that calls attention to and highlights certain hot spots on the body, most often the breast. This kind of erotica, created through iteration and reiteration (the nipple is echoed and repeated in such ornamentation as rubies, snowy pearls, daisies, diadems or pendants), builds to an erotic crescendo.

Far left, Titian, Girl in a Fur; *left, runway wedding dress; right, Bartolomeo Veneto,* Portrait of a Lady, *c. 1530*

*"When a civilized European woman
is naked in the presence of others,
her fundamental feeling seems
usually to be not 'I am ashamed
because I am naked,' but
'I am ashamed because I am
unadorned.' She feels, not that she
is revealing her beauty, but that
she is revealing herself deprived
of her weapons of seduction."*
—Havelock Ellis

● TOO HOT TO HANDLE   The highly orna-
mented woman can signal danger—as in
Klimt's interpretation of the biblical Judith
(1901), the seductive slayer of Holofernes.
The gold leaf that surrounds and adorns this
dark beauty produces a lurid iridescence
that heightens the warmth and sensuality of
her flesh. This painting came under fire in
its day for its overt erotic power.

● GLITTERING HOT AND COLD, draped onto
décolletage or winking from an earlobe,
gems are the most decadent form of erotic
adornment. When Tolstoy depicted a theater audience with "all the women with
gems on their bare flesh," he was offering
up a scene of sensual
opulence—an invitation
to a sexual feast.

Tintoretto, Portrait of a
Woman Revealing Her
Breasts

MAESTRA OF ORNAMENTAL SELF-DISPLAY, Elizabeth Taylor wears jewels as a kind of homage to her beauty, not least to accentuate her famous eyes and breasts.

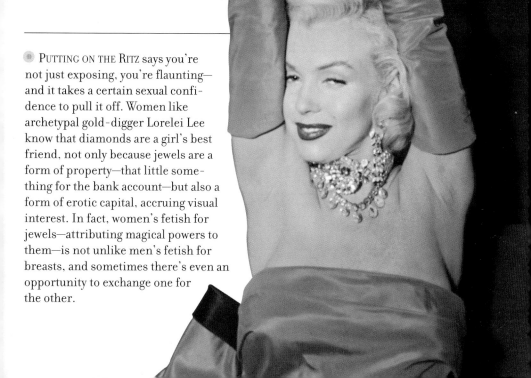

PUTTING ON THE RITZ says you're not just exposing, you're flaunting—and it takes a certain sexual confidence to pull it off. Women like archetypal gold-digger Lorelei Lee know that diamonds are a girl's best friend, not only because jewels are a form of property—that little something for the bank account—but also a form of erotic capital, accruing visual interest. In fact, women's fetish for jewels—attributing magical powers to them—is not unlike men's fetish for breasts, and sometimes there's even an opportunity to exchange one for the other.

"BREAST TATTOOS" once meant tattoos *of* breasts—jiggling on the flexed biceps of sailors, bikers and criminals. Loose women might get tattoos, but certainly nice girls didn't wear them—on the breast or anywhere else. But now women have taken on the tattoo as a form of personal expression. Little jokes or large decorative statements, tattoos can be as much an expression of sentiment and romance (a memory, a personal statement) as a primal declaration of erotic intention.

SPECIAL EFFECTS

Like seduction itself, simultaneously concealing and dramatizing, veiling is the art of synecdoche—where partial exposure stands for a larger whole. As if seen through a silk-covered camera lens, the shadowed breast glows, seems translucent and gives the suggestion of light without the fullness of exposure. Kept from us by a scrim of fabric, the veiled bosom creates an erotic distance, an illusion of perfection that we long to penetrate.

Right, Auguste Bernard, Lady Reading the Letters of Heloise and Abelard; *far right, Jacques-Louis David,* Portrait of a Young Woman in White

"He did not see her marble beauty forming a complete whole with her dress, but all the charm of her body only covered with her garments. And having once seen this he could not help being aware of it, just as we cannot renew an illusion we have once seen through."
—Leo Tolstoy, War and Peace

● THE DANCE OF THE SEVEN VEILS is not an ancient Middle Eastern tradition but the invention of playwright Oscar Wilde for his play *Salome*, loosely based on the biblical figure who demanded the head of John the Baptist on a plate. The infamous Salome and her seductive dance have become fixtures of erotica, inspiring a burlesque tradition and even interpretations by Isadora Duncan.

● SHADOW DANCE   Her figure is still, but the light trembling upon her skin seems to release the latent motion of her form. Grained like wood, but pulsing with life, her breasts, in their perfect shapeliness, have the power to bend light.

Man Ray, Retour
à la raison, *1923*

THEATER OF THE BEDROOM

When Jean Harlow asks in *Hell's Angels*, "Would you be shocked if I put on something more comfortable?" we know where things are heading. Seduction needs a stage set, and where better than the bedroom—a theater where breasts have a starring role in the evening's drama.

Dressing up to dress down, lingerie can be an elaborate costume that, unlike other forms of adornment, isn't a prelude to the action but part of the action itself. (Generally speaking, by the time you appear in a transparent nightie, it's

Right, Fredericks of Hollywood teddy

pretty clear where the evening will end.)
The pleasure can run both ways; putting
on a teddy is a kind of self-induced
foreplay. Satiny and ticklish, lingerie is
as much about texture for the wearer as
it is a visual for the lover—the firm hand
of underwire cupping the breast, the
prickle of lace on the nipple.

Between the sheets or on the streets,
women are more actively exploring their
own pleasure. Underwear has become
outerwear and the bedroom has entered
the larger world.

⬤ NIGHT CAP   Bettie Page, the cheese-
cake queen, invested each of her thou-
sands of pinup shots with a bit of theater.
With only a brief career in the 1950s
(beginning in magazines called *Wink*,
Eyeful and *Titter*), Page achieved status as
a cult icon, the full-figured poster girl for
naughty but nice. Whether posing in
fetish gear or as here, in lingerie, Page
used her costumes as props in a night-
time reverie.

LATEX is the new leather—a risqué second skin that makes it clear who's in control. If leather hints at the animal within, its synthetic cousin defies nature altogether. In this flexible fetish wear, women assert dominance in the act of seduction and self-display.

THE BIG TEASE

At the extreme end of adornment is the striptease, using veils, pasties and assorted costumes—all the tricks of the trade—to induce a brief and maddened state of excitation, mostly for male viewers. Focusing on the breasts (total nudity is still illegal in many places), the striptease plays with time, too, slowing down the removal of clothing in a gradual, calculated unveiling and compressing an entire courtship (if the end of courtship is undressing) into fifteen minutes. Of course, teasing is part of the stripping game, supplying the performance with its drama, though this is one occasion when we know we'll see what we paid for. In the traditional striptease, the breast is the final payoff.

Stripper Lee Sharon says, "Thank you all."

BIGGER, GLITZIER VERSIONS of what they cover, pasties amplify the nipple rather than conceal it. As illustrated by this wall mural, sometimes they can just be funny.

What Lies Beneath

Even the most decorous of interactions can involve a generalized sexual undertow, as the erotic mingles with our modest facades, if just for a moment. Think of the bra strap, peeking out from the shoulder; the shadow of a nipple hovering below the neckline. Half seen, just suggested, it is this moment between dressed and undressed, seen and unseen, where eros makes its home.

● SEXY IS confidence in casual display. When seventies rock beauty Bianca Jagger flashes her breasts under a veil—a disco-inspired netting—she shows just how little it takes to be a knockout.

AMERICAN ICON

"The mammary fixation is the most American of the sex fetishes."
—*Molly Haskell*

There is a strange and intimate connection between war and sex, and nothing expressed this better than the triumph of big breasts during World War II. Taped above bunks or passed on as creased mementos in battle theaters, wartime pinups literally buoyed the breasts, blowing them up to new proportions. Whether they meant red-bloodedness and patriotism or the apple-pie comforts of home, or were a virtual pillow for weary heads, men's desire for big breasts in times of conflict may be the result of instinctual longings. World War II soldiers craved milk, those at the front more than those nearer home.

"I Can Dream, Can't I?"
—*A GI escapes at naptime.*

THE PINUP

Women understood their new physical duties as part of the war effort. With armies of V-girls (V for Victory!) lifting spirits by entertaining troops on the "foxhole circuit," sex—or its suggestion—was a gesture of patriotism that women could make, too. In 1945, when the army sent Ralph Stein to Hollywood to photograph a series of pinups for the army, he found that the makeup women were more than used to augmenting bosoms, and in fact were keen to do more. He reported that during a debate over the number of felt pads to insert in a starlet's

sweater, one helper spoke for the rest: "What the hell, this is for the soldier boys— put three more pads over each breast."

Nothing spread the news of the new shape better than the GI mania for pinups. Trapped at the front lines, who could resist the bright-eyed charms of the girl whose accommodating curves promised everything waiting at home? Allied troops had first been introduced to sexy keepsakes with naughty postcards *(cartes postales suggestives)* found in Paris during World War I.

Even the phrase *pinup girl* was government-issue, having first appeared in the armed forces newspaper *Yank* on April 30, 1943. *Esquire* had featured its bosomy Petty Girl in the first 1933 issue and introduced its Varga Girl in 1940. Pinup prototypes had been seen in men's magazines before, but the unique combination of a captive audience and *Esquire*'s marketing savvy cemented the pinup's popularity. From 1942 to 1945, nearly 6 million free copies of *Esquire* were printed for American troops stationed abroad. When in 1944

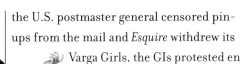

the U.S. postmaster general censored pin-ups from the mail and *Esquire* withdrew its Varga Girls, the GIs protested en masse.

SAVED BY THE BOSOM

For draftees, the memory of breasts could seem a kind of safe haven or virtual remedy. In the film *Saving Private Ryan*, a soldier recalls a woman showing him her sizable chest before he left for the front, saying: "When you're over there, if you see anything that upsets you, if you're ever scared, I want you to close your eyes and think of these."

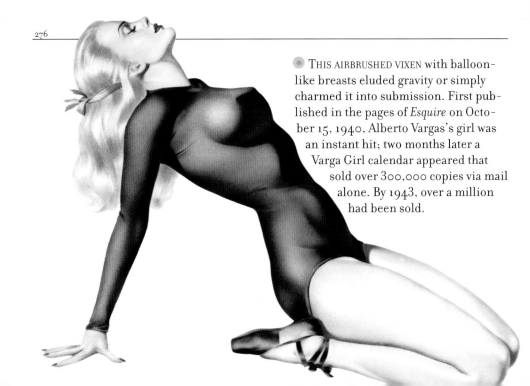

⬤ THIS AIRBRUSHED VIXEN with balloon-like breasts eluded gravity or simply charmed it into submission. First published in the pages of *Esquire* on October 15, 1940, Alberto Vargas's girl was an instant hit; two months later a Varga Girl calendar appeared that sold over 300,000 copies via mail alone. By 1943, over a million had been sold.

● NOSE ART   Pinups were totems of good luck, and what better place for them than the noses of U.S. bombers? Art historian Gary Vallant evoked a young soldier's obsession with these "painted ladies":

"It's midwinter, 1943, you're 20 years old . . . prior to December 1941, your main goal in life was to get a car and marry Ginger Rogers, but now it's just to stay alive another day because you're another crewman on a B-17, and where you're going people are going to die. But not you . . . not the special ones. They always come back. So we need a special name for our plane—and a special picture on it. Maybe a picture of Betty Grable, or one of those Varga Girls from Esquire."

BOMBER CREWS dubbed their aircraft with monikers—*Sack Time, Dragon Lady, Night Mission, Miss Laid, Lucky Strike*—that were loaded with sexual innuendo to match their pinup art.

BREASTS AND BOMBS remained culturally entangled: the bikini was named for the Pacific atoll where the Americans detonated an atomic bomb in 1946. Introducing his abbreviated two-piece bathing suit at a Paris fashion show four days after the explosion, designer Louis Réard said he chose the name because it perfectly expressed the idea of "the ultimate."

Munitions factory, 1943

BOMBSHELLS

While the war made pinups a booming business, Hollywood supported the war effort by turning its studio stars into pinup girls, sending starlets abroad on performing extravaganzas and distributing free prints of popular films to the troops. The Hollywood stars became national heroines and motion pictures became "as necessary to men as rations." The big breasts that symbolized patriotism would become a well-loved hallmark of the all-American girl.

The end of the war did not, however, deflate the American bosom. The postwar economic boom made *everything* explode, from birth rates to construction and the pumped-up curves of postwar car design—and breasts were bigger than they'd ever been.

● THE QUEEN OF WARTIME ENTERTAINMENT and star of the 1944 film *Pin Up Girl*, Betty Grable was voted the number-one pinup by GIs during World War II. Best known for her million-dollar legs, she also appealed to women, who were drawn to her sweet smile and natural wholesomeness.

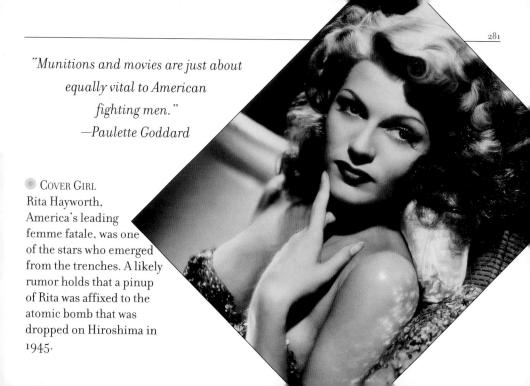

"Munitions and movies are just about equally vital to American fighting men."
—*Paulette Goddard*

● COVER GIRL
Rita Hayworth, America's leading femme fatale, was one of the stars who emerged from the trenches. A likely rumor holds that a pinup of Rita was affixed to the atomic bomb that was dropped on Hiroshima in 1945.

● THE BIG EASY   Advertising caught on to
the American spirit associated with healthy
chests. Fruit growers understood that breasts
were an excellent metaphor for tender
succulence—and patriotic consumption.

THE BRUNETTE

The early history of film is a battle between the plucky charms of the fair (like the girlish Mary Pickford) and the kohl-eyed insinuations of the vamp. Sylphlike and sinuous, dangerous femmes fatales like Theda Bara were known as much for their pool-like eyes as for the size of their bosoms. But in the golden age of cinema, during and after World War II, busty brunettes came to the fore. Led by lusty starlets like Jane Russell and Rita Hayworth, these women's missile-like bosoms pointed to a new, strong sexuality.

Right, Theda Bara in Cleopatra, *1917; far right, Clara Bow in* The Love Goddess, *1927 (pre–Production Code)*

SEX WAS IN FASHION after Freud introduced us to the primitive urges and the idea of "sexiness" was born. America's first "It" girl, Clara Bow wriggled her way into men's hearts. Before the restrictions of Hollywood's Production Code, these early starlets exposed more, though there was less to be exposed.

JANE RUSSELL, the prototype for the fast-talking, good-natured and bosomy brunette of the fifties, became a movie star of pinup order after her steamy appearance in *The Outlaw* (1946). Its skywriting publicity campaign was topped off by plumes of smoke in the shape of breasts. When the movie *The French Line* came out in 1954, Russell's double-D bosoms loomed even larger in 3-D.

Left, Gentlemen Prefer Blondes, *1953*

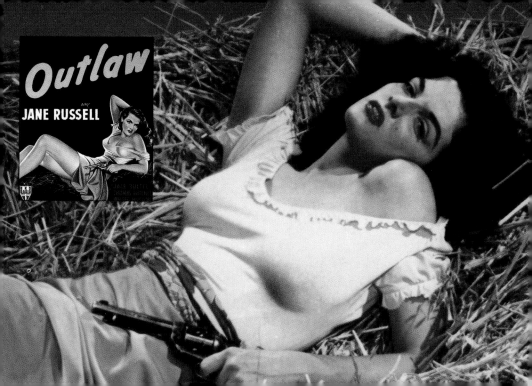

⬤ ELIZABETH TAYLOR'S DEEP CLEAVAGE seemed custom-made to set off the jewels she favored. With her violet eyes, wild fits of pique and matrimonial escapades, she matured into the regal chests of characters like Cleopatra, and the motherless bosom of Maggie in *Cat on a Hot Tin Roof*.

⬤ AVA GARDNER'S RIPE ASSETS made her into the Barefoot Contessa of fifties' Hollywood. Her vaguely ethnic beauty cast her in films as various as *The Night of the Iguana* and *Show Boat*, while her proud chest made her into a symbol of earthy glamour.

THE BLOND

Not all blonds are blond in fact. Although Betty Boop's hair remained black—restricted by black-and-white animation—at heart Betty's a blond, with her inviting babyishness (her "boo boo bee doop") and her shapely bosom. Blondness may well be a state of mind, and sexiness is at the heart of this blond appeal, an unthreatening and receptive allure accompanied by a plentiful bustline.

THE GREATEST ICON of twentieth-century blondness, Marilyn Monroe—with one flighty coo—broke a million hearts. Full-figured, with a bosom like a snowy pillow, Marilyn conveyed a brilliant and innocent sexuality. The woman loved by everyone, she always seemed to be singing "I Want to Be Loved by You," as in the 1959 film *Some Like It Hot* (right).

OUR FIRST "SWEATER GIRL," Lana Turner became a blond icon of buttoned-up sexuality whose fastenings, with the right prompting, just might burst.

A KIND OF ERSATZ MARILYN, Jayne Mansfield took blondness to a new extreme. In her first film, aptly titled *Female Jungle*, she played a nymphomaniac; her oft-displayed breasts came to seem like a literalization of sexual hopelessness. Publicity-hungry, she cultivated the exaggerated image of a sex goddess by owning a pink Hollywood mansion and jaguars.

"Too much of a good thing
is wonderful."
—Mae West

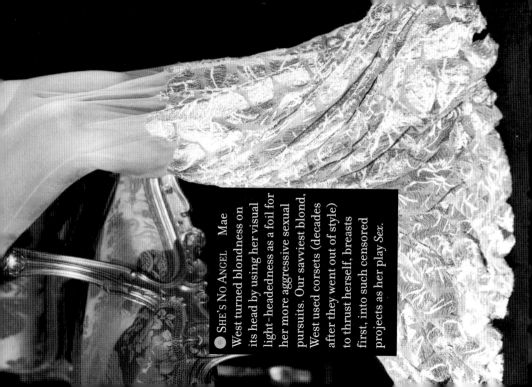

She's No Angel Mae West turned blondness on its head by using her visual light-headedness as a foil for her more aggressive sexual pursuits. Our savviest blond, West used corsets (decades after they went out of style) to thrust herself, breasts first, into such censored projects as her play *Sex*.

CLASS DISTINCTIONS

It may be harder today to recognize that breast size carries its former connotations of status and rank. Whether we've subconsciously held on to the class distinction, which originated from the upper classes' employing ample-breasted peasants as wet nurses, or harbor the fear of aging's effects, or adhere to the notion that discretion has its charms, we still associate small breasts with aristocratic severity and large breasts with the general populace. The rise of the model, a human clothes rack, has of course launched the fashion of almost no breasts at all.

A PATRICIAN BEAUTY, Katharine Hepburn chose roles that approximated her own affluent background, where her smart clothes' lines weren't marred by the appearance of a figure. Feline and angular, her kittenish good looks were offset by the austerity of her expression—and chest.

LIKE AN AFTERNOON LOVER, Audrey Hepburn projected a discreet sophistication. And her flat bosom made her a fashion designer's darling—as each tunic fell without interruption.

HITCHCOCK'S GOLDEN QUEEN, Grace Kelly was a paradigm of elegance. While she wasn't without breasts entirely, they were always understated—perhaps because nothing more needed to be said.

AN EROTIC PLAYGROUND, Anna Nicole Smith's chest won the attention and hand

of her former octo-genarian husband. Best known as a Guess jeans and *Playboy* model, Smith prominently displays her implants, letting us know how far she's gone to get here.

THE QUEEN OF COUNTRY, Dolly Parton is practically synonymous with her breasts. (Breasts have become known as "dollies," and the first cloned mammal was named Dolly for her genesis from a mammary gland.) A songbird from the mountains of Tennessee, she claims to have modeled herself after the town prostitute. Wondrous and tacky, she's her own creation of busty kitsch splendor.

HERE SHE COMES . . .

Beauty pageants, which offer scholarships, have often been the best way out for blossoming small-town girls. The first Miss America pageant, presenting the most democratic ideal of American beauty, was held in 1921; the creation of politicians and the media as a publicity campaign for Atlantic City, New Jersey, its mission was to discover a sweet, wholesome all-American girl. The first winner, Margaret Gorman (left), was only sixteen. Her measurements? 30-25-32.

1921

Forty-nine bathing beauties in a row, 1937

Contestants' figures have always played a deciding role, though not openly so. Initial criticism of the bathing suit competition caused the temporary closing of the contest in 1927. (There have been yearly calls to remove it ever after.) When the pageant was permanently resumed in 1935, a talent section was added to reassure the public that this was more than a body competition.

Over time, Miss Americas have reflected some of our nation's more modest ideals, and even the lineups' ampler chests seem more maternal than sexual. For while the participants have often reflected shapely trends, America's sweethearts avoid the suggestion that (as winners) they would offer anything more than a sweet smile for Mr. Right.

1954

Buxom Bunnies

aunched in 1953, Hugh Hefner's *Playboy* was marketed to the young, upwardly mobile men who constituted the postwar boom's freshman class. *Playboy* cannily mixed nudity and niceness; Hefner's Playmates were presented as girls next door who just happened to be naked, with autobiographical sketches that voiced their wholesome middle-class aspirations. The formula worked, and *Playboy*'s success made history: circulation per issue went from 1 million in 1960 to 6 million at the end of the decade.

● "A GAY NINETIES rig that exaggerated their hips, bound their waists in a ceinture, and lifted them into a phallic brassiere," wrote Norman Mailer about the bunny costume after visiting the first Playboy Club. "Each breast looked like the big bullet on the front bumper of a Cadillac."

MADE IN THE USA

Although pornography preceded implants, large breasts weren't always the erotic foci they are today; in some historical periods, the bottom was the preferred enlarged body part. Two products, however, have made porno and breasts literally and metaphorically "bigger": silicone and home videos. In the United States, augmented breasts dominate pornography, and triple-X films feature triple-D breasts.

Why is it that supersized breasts seem an insult to our intelligence? Breasts that are almost (if not actually) bigger than a

woman's head are not only the largest statement on her body, but the defining one, communicating to men, "I'm available, for fun, with payment and without conditions." Of course, the stigma attached to this kind of sexual purchase—where sex is an open exchange of commerce, rather than intimacy—makes consumers want to degrade the object of purchase as well.

● SMOTHER ME   Aptly named actress Chesty Morgan plays a murderer in *Deadly Weapons* with bad mothering instincts—her victims are suffocated between her breasts.

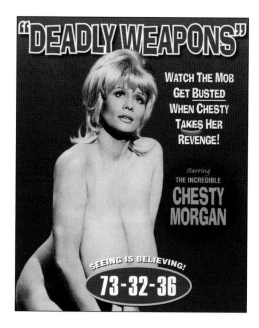

NOVELTIES

The golden age of goofy gender jokes was the fifties and sixties—before the sexual revolution stamped them out. Risqué and relatively harmless, kitsch at its most ordinary, these objects herald a middle-class world where naughtiness is drunk with a double martini on your Formica bar.

BOOBY PRIZE   Artifacts of pre-PC mass culture, these joke gifts make men as well as breasts into cartoons.

a Cigarette Holder

Get the full ...ption

...s to be different

Have one!

MARTINI CUPS show just how intoxicating breasts can be. Like the nursing lid and cigarette holders, these novelties point to breasts' addictive properties, or the desire to simply drink deep.

IT'S MOUTH WATERING!

NURSE YOUR DRINK

...tch · Bourbon

NURSE YOUR DRINK

NURSE YOUR DRINK

A GIRL'S BEST FRIEND

The great American icon. Barbie was placed in the 1976 bicentenary time capsule—and time will tell that she has yet another plastic advantage over the rest of us: her breasts will never sag. Or, as M. G. Lord wrote in *Barbie Forever:* "She can never bloat. She has no children to betray her. Nor can she rot, wrinkle, overdose or go out of style."

Sears initially found Barbie too sexy to stock. But little girls everywhere fell in love with the cool blond with moving parts, even though they knew they would never measure up. Barbie's companions have mostly

● DESEXING OF BARBIE was intentional. Nipples that appeared on early prototypes were filed off with emery boards.

suffered by comparison: her younger sister, Skipper, got to hope for sexual maturity, even if it was in a perpetual cycle. "Growing up Skipper" had breasts that grew as her arm was turned.

A mute ideal for the Girl Who Had Everything, including boys' hearts, Barbie became not only the star of playtime but, for adults living with her legacy, shorthand for girlish vapidity. (Gloria Steinem was once called a "counterculture Barbie doll.")

● BLAST FROM THE PAST   Barbie's pre-fabricated curves have an unexpectedly international and slightly sordid history. Ruth Handler, a co-founder of Mattel,

Wer mit Liebe schenkt — an Lilli denkt

No. 1113A

Neuheit!
Novelty!
Nouveauté!

modeled Barbie on Lilli, a German doll marketed to men—part of a long Continental tradition of pornographic miniatures. With the help of Japanese manufacturers, Barbie was launched in 1959, a close replica of the Lilli doll with softer features and a new all-American charm.

5'8"

36"

18"

22"

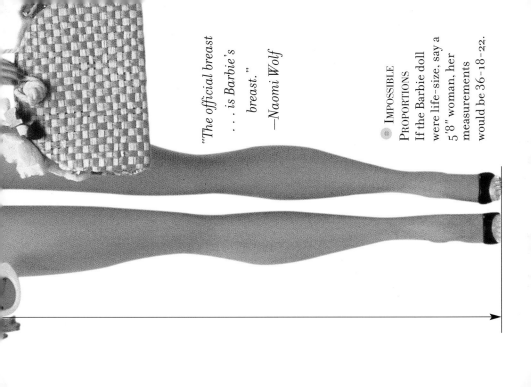

"The official breast . . . is Barbie's breast."
—Naomi Wolf

● IMPOSSIBLE
PROPORTIONS
If the Barbie doll
were life-size, say a
5'8" woman, her
measurements
would be 36–18–22.

MILITANT EXPOSURE

"The breast is mightier than the sword."
—*Anonymous*

From the Amazons onward, the bared breast of the warrior woman has stood for defiance. Self-exposure is a title of self-ownership, a badge of strength that suggests danger and puts men on guard. This attention-grabbing eyeful is disruptive to our sense of social order and of things being where they belong. Displayed pridefully in public, remote from their nurturing or erotic functions, breasts can project an unfamiliar power—one of raw femininity unleashed.

Attack of the 50 Ft. Woman, *1958—If her breasts aren't big enough, her height will show them who's boss.*

WOMEN WARRIORS

Homer called Amazons "women the equal of men." Though these "golden-shielded, silver-sworded, man-loving" women emerged from ancient myth, their fighting spirit makes us wish they really had existed. Named for their distinctive anatomy (in Greek, *a* = without, *mastos* = breast), Amazons seared off one breast in childhood so they could draw their bows unimpeded and allow more strength to flow into the bow-pulling arm. Some legends say they sought out men only once a year, to conceive the girl children who would carry on their mighty tradition, and

otherwise kept men at arm's (or sword's) length. Showing neither the modesty nor reticence firmly demanded of their real-life Athenian counterparts, Amazon women projected an erotic appeal that could not be civilized in marriage. Their signature monomastia represented their freedom from conventional maternal obligations and attachments to the opposite sex.

THE ORIGINAL GOOD BAD GIRLS, Amazons turned Greek warriors into the first boy toys. The best weapon in the Amazon's arsenal was her lone breast, exposed on the battlefield against men in full armor.

WONDER WOMAN'S strapping resemblance to an Amazon isn't coincidental. In the 1950s, anti-comic crusader Frederic Wertham claimed (amazingly!) that her proud breasts inspired lesbianism: "for girls, she is a morbid ideal. Her followers are the gay girls."

THE AMAZON IMAGE,
whether classically sculpted in
marble or admired today in the
flesh-and-blood form of warrior
princess Xena, is sensual, capti-
vating and armed for the kill.

THE GODDESS ARTEMIS was devoutly worshiped by the Amazons, who were believed to have honored her by building her temple at Ephesus—known in the ancient world as one of the seven wonders. Her many-breasted majesty celebrates female fertility and autonomy.

THE STORY OF ST. AGATHA

The legend of the beautiful Agatha dates to the third century A.D., when this pious virgin, daughter of a distinguished Sicilian family, spurned the sexual advances of the Roman senator Quintianus. Quintianus had her breasts cut off—a cruel order that furnished later painters with a gruesomely fascinating subject. Though Agatha was miraculously healed by a vision of St. Peter, she eventually died at the hands of her torturers.

Right, Piombo, Martyrdom of St. Agatha; *far right, Zurbarán,* Saint Agatha

AS IF SERVING CUPCAKES on a tray (right), St. Agatha assumes a hostesslike pose that alarms modern viewers but was once typical of martyrs displaying the objects of their torture. Her placid demeanor expresses her divinely inspired strength.

BREASTS ON THE FRONT LINES

Without literally taking up arms, women have engaged in protest by using their bared breasts.

When Lady Godiva accepted a dare from her husband, Earl Leofric, to ride her horse naked through the streets of Coventry in opposition to his oppressive taxation, she fired more women's imaginations than men's. The townspeople, honoring her modesty and courage, shut themselves behind closed shutters as she rode—except for one young tailor, dubbed "Peeping Tom," who dared to take a gander and was, the story goes, struck blind as a result. So filled with admiration was Godiva's husband that upon her return he granted the people a charter of freedom.

● LADY GODIVA'S FAMOUS RIDE let other women know that they possessed significant clout beneath their bodices. Her own nakedness resulted in a political victory for the people of Coventry.

"A woman can still be beautiful and can wear her scars as a symbol of strength."
—Matuschka

Photographer Matuschka's postmasectomy self-portrait, Beauty Out of Damage, appeared on the cover of The New York Times Magazine, August 15, 1993.

Breasts have been bared in defense of choice and in support of increased funding for breast cancer. Strictly speaking, such exposure violates U.S. law, but while women have been arrested for breast-feeding in public, these media-grabbing demonstrations have not drawn police action.

In 1998, covered up yet equally striking in their silence, victims of silicone implants held a candlelight vigil in front of the White House. "This is our way of showing that we have survived this tragedy," said one spokesperson, "even if it is still in our thoughts."

COURAGE UNDER FIRE

Even the deeply religious Sojourner Truth, antislavery activist and former slave, bared her breast to a white audience in 1858 when challenged by a group of pro-slavery men to prove her claims to womanhood—as if it were mascu-

line to protest. She observed that it was to their shame, not hers, that she uncovered her breast.

As baring the breast became a frequent strategy for demonstrators, the U.S. Army Military Police included this scenario in their pamphlet to prepare the troops:

Situation: You are in formation faced by a group of females about your age. They yell: "If you are on our side, smile" and then raise their blouses to expose their breasts. How do you handle this?

Solution: Concentrate on what you're there for. After all, you've seen breasts before. The girls are just teasing and want you to make a mistake so they can ridicule you. Stay sharp and alert!

BARRED FROM BARING THEIR BREASTS in public, Canadian women (right) crossed into New York State, where a Buffalo judge had recently authorized the right to go topless.

TOPLESS IN WASHINGTON, D.C., for a 1971 antiwar demonstration, this naughty protestor garbed herself in the Stars and Stripes and raised a bottle of cheap wine in place of the lamp of freedom.

LET 'EM LOOSE

Long before bras went up in flames, women used their undergarments as symbols of their oppression. Nineteenth-century feminists railed against the corset, though respectable women weren't yet ready to let 'em loose.

When the sexual revolution and the feminist "second wave" coincided in the 1960s, the bra became an icon of sexual and social restraint. This time women were ready to unhook—in large numbers and in prominent places.

The "braless" look made a new fashion statement—though not always a comfortable

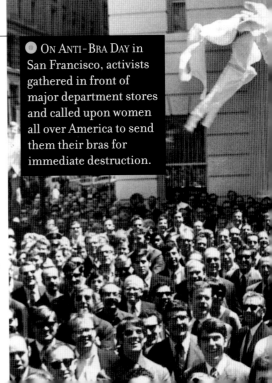

● ON ANTI-BRA DAY in San Francisco, activists gathered in front of major department stores and called upon women all over America to send them their bras for immediate destruction.

one. This underwear rebellion favored the less well endowed, and large breasts were considered by many feminists more a bane than an asset; Germaine Greer noted that "a full bosom is actually a millstone around a woman's neck." Chucking the form-fitted look for a loose and pendulous liberty was a signal to men that women would no longer perpetuate, as Greer put it, "the fantasy of pneumatic boobs." Going braless not only released women from conforming to the *Playboy*-inspired male fantasy but also signaled freedom—on their own terms.

LADIES LIBERTY:
BARING IT FOR THE NATION

When used to personify the motherland, women's bodies literally draw us to the bosom of the country. While America's Columbia, Britain's Britannia and Prussia's Germania were all modeled on the sagacious, proud and warlike goddess Athena, the most lasting symbol of statehood came with the birth of the French Republic. In Delacroix's famous portrayal, *Liberty Leading the People*, the "mother" in motherland took on new meaning with Liberty's breasts bursting free of her bodice. Her deshabille symbolized the natural claims of liberty, equality and fraternity, as well as duty and valiant sacrifice.

Although art historian Anne Hollander described Delacroix as "the greatest Romantic expositor of complex passion through mammary exposure," Liberty herself was not free from scandal; the rumor is that Delacroix's model was a Parisian prostitute. And in 1978, when she and her swollen breasts appeared on 100-franc notes, the notes were deemed so indecent in some countries that they were refused exchange.

Eugene Delacroix, Liberty Leading the People, *1830*

THE ROMAN LIBERTY (right) is clearly reflected in Ingres's nineteenth-century Joan of Arc. With crosses for nipples, Joan's armor suggestively mimics Liberty's bared bosom.

⬤ LIBERTY FOR ALL   In many images, Liberty's breasts are meant to show the nation's nurturing intentions. Here she sits with stalwart dignity, suckling her people and equally accessible to all. (The conventional French disdain for breast-feeding was temporarily suspended during the Revolution when mothers enthusiastically nursed their infants as their patriotic duty.)

LIBERTY, EQUALITY, 36C

In the 1850s, the female embodiment of liberty was finally named: Marianne was probably a code word for "revolution." A busty presence in city halls throughout France, Marianne took her looks from the services of local models until 1969, when the town of Thiron-Gardais displayed a bust modeled on Brigitte Bardot, who, despite some bureaucratic dissent, served as the de facto symbol of the French Republic until 1985.

● UNDERWEAR MODEL Laetitia Casta is selected as the "Millennial Marianne" by a nationwide vote of French mayors. Modeling the national icon on the current heartthrob has sparked controversy.

LADY LIBERTY (France's gift to her sister republic) is the female answer to Uncle Sam. This shapely version by Samuel George Phillips, painted in 1910, is neither militaristic nor maternal. Here she looks heavenward, but wartime incarnations would direct their gaze at the viewer, imploring men to protect the nation's honor or urging the purchase of war bonds. By World War II, images of "real" American women—Red Cross nurses, Wacs, Waves, and wholesome wives and daughters—replaced Liberty as the national poster girl.

LIBERTY AS SEXPOT Italian porn star and political candidate La Cicciolina campaigned with bare breasts and arm raised in anticipation of her triumph. She was elected to parliament in 1987, on the platform: "Say no to sexual repression!"

KINDER, GENTLER BREASTS

From militancy and protest to liberation and national pride, the bared breast has had many different meanings. It can also be a symbol of charity or supplication, a female relinquishment of power. In Homer's *Iliad*, Hecuba bares her breast to her son Hector, imploring him not to fight the much-feared Achilles—who ultimately vanquishes him.

Charity exposes her breast to feed a helpless man.

Pointing to her exposed breast, the desperate mother declares, "Hector, my child! Look—have some respect for *this*! Pity your mother, too, if I ever gave you the breast to soothe your troubles, remember it now, dear boy."

In a moment's reprieve from the national and gender wars, the baring of the breast can also express playful disinhibition, girlish freedom and sisterly exuberance, as in Picasso's *Deux femmes courant sur la plage* (right).

WE'LL SHOW 'EM!

"I sometimes see men walking around publicly bare-chested, often with fleshy stomachs hanging over their trousers. It always amazes me to witness their seeming sense of comfort with their bodies. . . . I feel awe at the courage of these [women] artists who stripped bare in front of their mirrors to confront and depict the reality of female flesh."
—Judy Chicago

Just as taking your shirt off in front of other women is nothing like taking it off in a room full of men, the intended audience makes a difference in portrayals of nudes in paintings and photographs. Until the twentieth century, both the artist and the audience were generally men, and the female nude (especially the bosom) was restricted to their domain. Now women are taking up the brush and camera to shed new light on the female body, mainly for their own pleasure but often with the tradition of male viewing in mind.

Previous page,
Mary Ellen Mark;
right, Lisa Yuskavage,
Northview, *2000*

"Women are depicted [by male artists] in quite a different way—not because the feminine is different from the masculine—but because the 'ideal' spectator is always assumed to be male and the image of the woman is designed to flatter him."
—John Berger

A NEW POINT OF VIEW

In one way or another, women artists are reclaiming their breasts. Sometimes the aim is to reorient male attitudes or just to explore their own feelings about breasts or femininity in general. Sometimes the statement is an irritable if not angry parody of the male tradition of idealized breasts—a demand that we take a good look at some real-life ones. Some artists are just poking fun at men's obsession with the double mounds of womanhood ("You want to see breasts? I'll show you breasts!"). Others have magnified the power of breasts, making of them a kind of feminine phallus. Still others have appreciated their formal beauty (minus the erotic charge) or tried to reestablish breasts' place at the heart of their owners' sensual lives. And sometimes they've decorated them just for fun.

⬤ THE GREAT MULTIMAMMIA   Louise Bourgeois's humorous reprise of Diana of Ephesus presents a deadpan, modern-day goddess, armless but wielding a powerful sense of irony.

REVISITING THE CLASSICS

W omen artists have taken on the idealized breast images by the great masters and given them a makeover, and no one does it more joltingly than Cindy Sherman. As model and photographer, she assembles herself and her setting with deliberate haphazardness to showcase the sheer constructedness of past female images, art's myths of femininity.

With her Madonnas' "fake tits" (as she calls them), Sherman re-creates religious scenes from masterworks, stripping them of the spiritual power that lent meaning to their strange configuration. In classic paintings, the "holy breast" offered to the Christ child is often oddly disfigured and centered, and the Virgin's posture is revealed to be forced and stylized. Seen through Sherman's eyes, the Renaissance breast appears to have been insincerely sanctified—and perhaps exposed for less than godly reverence.

CINDY SHERMAN'S regal Madonna pastiches early Renaissance Madonnas like that of Jean Fouquet (far right and right, respectively). Both posture and coloring give Sherman a modern doll-like look, her plastic breast matching her plastic infant.

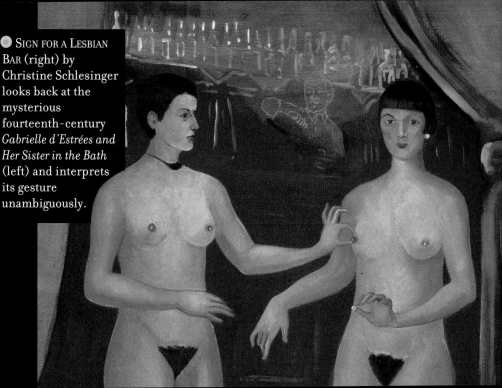

SIGN FOR A LESBIAN BAR (right) by Christine Schlesinger looks back at the mysterious fourteenth-century *Gabrielle d'Estrées and Her Sister in the Bath* (left) and interprets its gesture unambiguously.

LOOKING SQUARELY AT MYSELF

*"Men look at women. Women
watch themselves being looked at."*
—John Berger

The female artist has learned to stare back, to turn her gaze onto the world and herself, becoming, as Alice Neel commented, "someone who looks . . . somebody who inspects, somebody who scrutinizes." In these searching self-portraits, the goal seems to be self-examination, a good, hard, honest look that doesn't pass judgment. Taking on the nude tradition in which men painted and women posed, the artists occupy both roles at once. They are their own models, and for them nakedness is neither vulnerable nor shameful nor decorative. Instead, we find a bracing reverie on selfhood, where sex is taken as one of the body's moods—not its character. These are bodies with history; unlike idealized nudes, they have lived lives.

● ARTIST AND NUDE are usually on opposite ends of the canvas, one looking, the other looked at, but Charlotte Berend-Corinth brings the model next to her in a mirrored image. For once we see the two together, as if working side by side.

Breast sizes have sometimes been associated with particular social classes where
larger usually means lower. British photographer Jo Spencer, who works in a kind of
"photo-theater," comments on this tradition
of classification by breast size and shape in
Colonization. Posing herself naked with her
pendulous "working-class" breasts, she's at
once a "breast-feeder" and a bared "native"
captured by the white man's camera. In this
double context her message is clear: both are
women whose breasts have been classified,
colonized and exploited.

Suzanne Valadon, former circus acrobat, model for Renoir and Toulouse-Lautrec, and mother of Maurice Utrillo, here paints herself in a bare-breasted self-portrait (1917). Seizing the initiative, she records the elegant angularity and roundness—severity and softness—that constitute her beauty.

● *BIRTHDAY*   Surrealism meets film noir in Dorothea Tanning's 1942 self-portrait. In this dreamscape, with its infinite recess of doors and her tendriled skirt, the painter's bared breasts seem like an isolated reprieve from hallucination—a touch of the glorious real.

● *NUDE SELF-PORTRAIT*   An aging Alice Neel presents her breasts with blithe and prosaic simplicity, brushing off any kudos for her courage and frankness. Of the 1980 painting she said, "my own face bores me. . . . But with the whole body, there are strange things going on—the flesh is falling off the bones. . . . I have a prehensile big toe and there's a leg that as a leg is frightful, but as a work of art, it's gorgeous."

"Who the hell do you think you're kidding, Grobwitz?"

SEX OBJECTS

Just as women have often been treated like objects, so have their breasts—as if only they, not their owners, were worthy of attention. Mocking the breasts' objectlike status, artists have plopped them into unexpected contexts to create comedy or shake things up. And sometimes breasts take on a life independent of their owners.

● *PLAYBOY* CARTOONS tend to make more fun of men than of women, especially of men's helplessness before breasts. In this comic, erotic universe, breasts are the accidental perpetrators of a single victimless crime: masculine self-abasement.

ARTEMIS BLANKET Is this cozy comforter designed for male or female cuddling? Merrilee Challiss summons an assortment of associations: the 1930s-style bed frame brings Edward Hopper's stark urban nudes to mind, except that here the Hopper nude is replaced by tidy rows of breasts. More creepily, the title's invocation of the huntress Artemis makes us wonder if she's been tamed—and skinned like a tiger rug.

● *STILL LIFE* Jo Spencer's consumer breasts, like the chickens and giblets beside them, have been relegated to the meat section. The once "sacred cows" are here reduced to shelf goods with a price tag, on sale for cheap.

● *BREAST JAR* (right), by Kiki Smith, highlights the breast's subjection to science, to surgeries and high-powered technologies. Like the classic sci-fi brain floating in a mystery liquid (perhaps still thinking its helpless thoughts), the breast appears to be a victim of foul play.

● *ONE IS NOT ENOUGH, THREE ARE TOO MANY*
With these party-time accessories,
Maureen Connnor suggests breasts' power
of intoxication and the 1960s-style
debonair bachelor who, in his swanky
bachelor pad, plied martinis (perhaps
instead of sexual talent) to loosen female
inhibition.

BODY ART

In the early 1960s, artists began to use their bodies as an extended medium, creating actions and performances that shocked the public into confronting their attitudes toward female sexuality in general and breasts in particular. As artist Cheri Gaulke observed, "Performance is not a difficult concept for women. We're onstage every moment of our lives. In performance, we found an art form that was young—without conventions established by men. The shoe fit, and so like Cinderella we ran with it."

Breasts, the most malleable members of the body, have been playfully transformed, defying their sexual and nurturing functions or just highlighting their distinctive formal properties. Body art in this instance does more than decorate; it teases and tweaks our on-again, off-again reverence for the female anatomy. Here, neither modesty nor nature rules; breasts can be funny—and why shouldn't they be?

BOSOM BALLET Ex–porn star, filmmaker Annie Sprinkle's breasts put on a show of their own—clever girls—with a little guidance from their black-gloved sidekicks. In the live stage performance of the piece, they dance to "The Blue Danube."

WE'VE ALL ENCOUNTERED the "checking them out" look—the man's stare that locks onto our chests and can hardly be coaxed back up to meet our eyes. For her work of feminist guerrilla art, *Tap and Touch Cinema* (right), VALIE EXPORT invited random men on the street to place their hands inside the curtained box to fondle her breasts. The one catch: they had to look her in the eye for the duration. The exercise placed the male participant in the unusual position of receiving the returned gaze of his anonymous sex object. Nevertheless, it looks like a friendly exchange.

Left, playful body painters turn down the volume on breasts' sexual signal.

MY MOTHER / MYSELF

Mothers and daughters are as familiar with each other's bodies as they are fascinated by them; they literally embody for one another what was, what might have been, what will be. Their mutual scrutiny, at times a point of friction ("Why on earth are you wearing that?"), can also open the artist to an unexplored world of mutual female understanding, as daughters and mothers look upon each other as no one else can. Between these two, the breast is the literal point of contact. The nursing mother, glorified for centuries in Christian art, has

been recast by women artists like Mary Cassatt, with a focus on the physical bonds. Childless herself, Cassatt took mothers and daughters as her primary theme, portraying these young nurturers as strong yet gentle, solid yet sensual.

Mary Cassatt, Mother Rose
Nursing Her Child

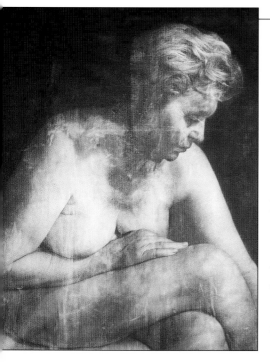

Contemporary painterly photographer Melanie Manchot has unsentimentally taken her mother as the principal subject of her work, drawing on the intimacy achievable only between mother and daughter. While some artists have pre-sented aging women as a feminist challenge to received ideas of feminine beauty, Manchot is intrigued by her mother's body as both familiar and exotic. It is her past, the place she came from, the breasts she suckled, and it is also her future—the body she will grow to resemble. She refers to her mother as Mrs. Manchot in all her titles.

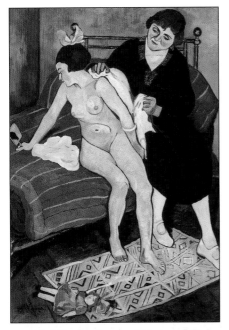

As DAUGHTERS GROW UP and develop sexually, mothers may feel they are handing over to them their own erotic power. In Suzanne Valadon's *The Abandoned Doll* (1921), the round-breasted daughter, on the threshold of womanhood, exchanges her doll for a mirror, as, perhaps, her mother has exchanged her youthful charms for maternal love.

MY NANNY AND I   Drawing on the rich symbolism of the Mexican tradition, Frida Kahlo explored the theme of maternity in cosmic terms with the nursing breast, its ducts and glands exposed, mirroring the natural landscape. Painted at a point when she was mourning her own childlessness, the picture shows Kahlo being nourished by the natural resources of her ancestors. When she was a child, her nurse told her that "rain was the milk of the Virgin."

EROS

Studies have shown that erotic images of women are arousing to other women as well as to men—and that even for heterosexual women they are more stirring than male erotic nudes. When these images are created by female artists, breast size is not proportionate to sexual allure, and breasts can become integrated into the lyrical rhythms of the body—diffusing the erotic zones. Identifying with the image to the point of entering it, these women feel the breasts' curves as perhaps only a woman can.

◉ *LES DEUX AMIES*   The shadowy drama of erotic friendship is intensified in this 1923 work by Tamara de Lempicka. The Art Deco sleekness of the duo highlights not only curves but the almost electric surface of their flesh—and the charge between them.

◉ *TRIANGLES*   Exploring the dynamic between curve and angle, Imogen Cunningham shows that the erotic tilts at 45 degrees. The triangle of the breast is reiterated throughout the composition—in the nipple, and in the negative space behind—proving that the female body, even when partially abstracted, loses none of its magnetic allure.

Güler Uğer, nude, 1999

"*When I photograph a woman nude, I'm curious; I want to capture her. When a male photographer sees a woman nude, he wants to possess her.*"

—Güler Uğer

● *GraceLynn Lying Down*, Emily Simpson's alluring study of a nude, reveals the unenhanced beauty of the body as a restfully alert presence. This breast's distinctiveness breaks from cliché and suggests the intimacy of revealing what is genuinely personal.

● In *Duo*, the women's bodies radiate a joyous sexuality. Painter Lorraine Inzalaco celebrates her love for women, making the lesbian experience visible—to claim and enjoy.

PLEASURES OF THE FLESH

De Kooning once said, "Flesh was the reason why oil painting was invented." In idealized nudes, breasts are often the only fleshy feature of the female nude, but for artists who have taken a painterly pleasure in feminine corpulence, much of the body becomes breastlike— soft, pliable, undulating.

British artist Jenny Saville specializes in oversize female bodies that she paints big. In *Branded*, far right (the painting towers seven feet high), Saville

Flesh is infernal in this detail from Rubens's Dante's Inferno.

experiments with language, carving words associated with traditional femininity— "supportive," "delicate," "decorative," terms defied by her subject's proportions and personality—into both the paint and, it seems, the flesh. Saville tries to twist the signs and codes of the nude tradition in order to, as she writes, "keep the language alive." And indeed we encounter a nude with weighty, in-your-face breasts that bust the mold.

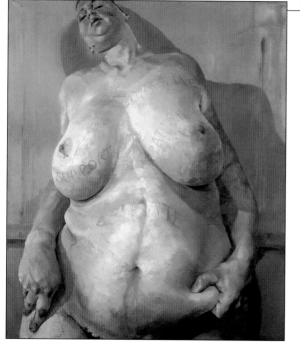

"I'm interested in the physical
power a large female body
has—a body that occupies a lot
of physical space, but also
someone who's acutely aware
that our contemporary culture
encourages her to disguise
her bulk and look
as small as possible."
—Jenny Saville

WARM, ALMOST GLOWING, Vanessa Bell's *Nude* (1922) conveys the some-how fragile nature of this sturdily built woman as well as her trust in the artist. Her breasts' asymmetry suggests not their imperfection but their material substance, the way they feel to their owner: weighty, tugging, and resting upon the flesh beneath.

ALL CARTOON BREASTS and blurred faces, Lisa Yuskavage's women are as fleshy as the boudoirs in which they're found lounging—unfurled bosoms waiting for the touch of troubled hands. Bad beauty queens, or good escorts, these are women as flowers—whose bloom is quickly passing.

TENDER ADDRESS

"I touched her sleeping breasts,
and they opened to me suddenly
like spikes of hyacinth."
—Federico García Lorca, *"The Faithless Wife"*

Couple in bath, fifteenth-century German woodcut

The fit between hand and breast may not be perfect, but once transformed into that of caresser and caressed, it's a match made in heaven. To touch the breast, or allow it to be touched, is to cross a threshold into a new realm of trust, intimacy—and heat. That small embrace evokes other feelings, from tenderness to the laying of claim on the part of the giver. Touching the breasts is a crucial part of foreplay—playing with the breasts' capacity for arousal. Here, as lovers ease into an embrace, giving and taking become one and the same.

BREASTS CALL OUT to be cupped, their softness seeking fleshly support, and the hand is happy to comply.

FIRST EXPLORATIONS

A girl can go many years before her breast is ever touched by a hand other than her own, and she'll never forget those first tentative, fumbling fingers or their fondling owner: where they were and how she felt about it. Later memories may include another charged first: that moment during nursing when her baby reaches up for a second point of connection. This hand-breast contact leaves another set of fingerprints. Still, there comes the day when the mother will say a gentle no to that hand, and it will have to seek out others, elsewhere.

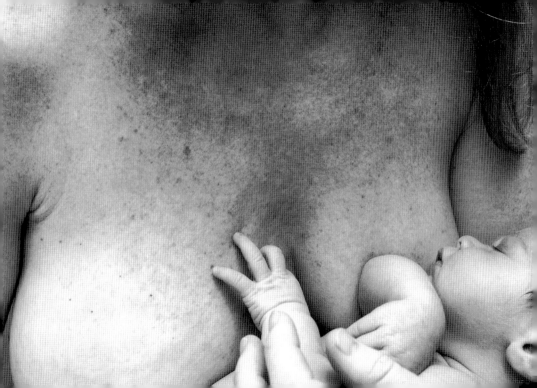

BABY-FACED CUPID seizes the breast of his mother Venus in a no-longer-infantile grasp in the complex *Allegory of Love*, a sixteenth-century painting by Bronzino.

"License my roving hands,
and let them go,
Before, behind, between,
above, below."
—John Donne,
"To His Mistress Going to Bed"

Copping a Feel

The breast is the first place a sweetheart can touch that's not part of the public repertoire of affection. Whether granted as a privilege or favor, whether bought or stolen, the "copped" feel has the kick of transgression—the hand caught in the cookie jar. The pleasure can be mutual or, like a pinch on a crowded bus, entirely one-sided. It's not called "second base" for nothing; the player is halfway there, his sights set on reaching home.

● FEELING UP   In paintings by Otto Dix and Picasso, the men are taking matter in hand.

HANDS-ON JUDGES at Rio de Janeiro's Carnival measure more than looks. They're feeling out fit as well as form.

COUPLING

All lovers engage in the same broad scenario: two characters enacting a drama where their desires and hopes are literally expressed in the handling of each other's bodies. Even amid the fiery absolutes of passion, there are many ways to touch and be touched, from the mastering grasp to the provocative pinch. Perhaps, like Sethe in Toni Morrison's *Beloved*, you want to give yourself over—"What she knew was that the responsibility for her breasts, at last, was in somebody else's hands"—or to be taken in hand and finally held still. Perhaps you want to offer up the comfort of your flesh or be comforted yourself. The breast, fondly touched, can be the key to unlocking a woman's feelings.

Left, eleventh-century Indonesian statue of Vishnu and Lakshmi

● LOVE, OLYMPUS-STYLE Artists often use mythical lovers to depict otherwise forbidden scenes of physical passion. As in Boucher's *Hercules and Omphale*, the gods provide the mortal viewer with earthly inspiration.

● ACCORDING TO MYTH, Cupid would disappear if Psyche ever looked at him, so the lovers met only in darkness. Of this statue, in which Cupid seems pretty adept at feeling his way around in the dark, Gustave Flaubert wrote: "I looked at nothing else in the gallery. I returned to it several times and at last kissed the armpit of the swooning woman. . . . May I be forgiven. It was my first sensual kiss in a long while."

BEAUTY AND THE BEAST

Presenting a perfect picture of impossible longing, the beast is easier to understand than the beauty in this story of unlikely attraction. As he yearns to be transformed into a real lover, to relinquish his ferocity and be tamed, he's also longing for the milk of human love.

If she reciprocates, the maiden tells a different story. In her engagement, she represents a feminine longing to let loose the beast in herself, to be—if not literally—manhandled.

● GENTLE GIANT   In this 1976 remake of the thirties classic, King Kong gently lifts a terrified Jessica Lange for a closer look. A glimpse of her breast may have been just too unsettling for the smitten beast; in any case, this risqué vignette didn't make it to the final cut.

TO HAVE AND TO HOLD

Married love is harder to characterize, lacking the charge of illicit love or first encounters. But while this is not the embrace of stolen moments, domestic attachment has its own poetry. What we rarely see in the public sphere is this ordinary gesture of prolonged intimacy and earned entitlement: a hand that has molded over time into a practiced cupping—a perfect fit. Closest to the heart, the wifely breast becomes a literal touchstone for the husband.

Left, Rembrandt van Rijn, The Jewish Bride; *right, Titian,* Allegory of Married Life

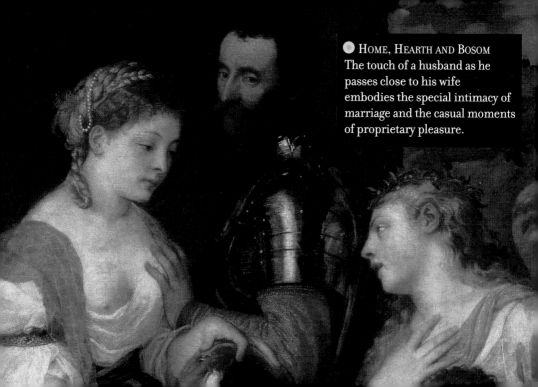

HOME, HEARTH AND BOSOM
The touch of a husband as he passes close to his wife embodies the special intimacy of marriage and the casual moments of proprietary pleasure.

ME, MYSELF . . . MINE

One of our most automatic gestures is putting a hand to our breast: it's the "Who, me?" of surprise, the "Oh, no" of instant denial, the showing of

modesty or tender feeling—after all, we're in the region of the heart. But aside from the vital routine of medical self-examination, women have few occasions to wrap their hands around

their own breasts. When we lift them to enjoy their weight and feel, displaying them on the platter of our palms, it's usually not even for ourselves. But a self-caress can hold ourselves in check or let us explore our own feelings, emotional or physical, *and* sensual.

● THE SHADOW OF A HAND poignantly defines the ghostly presence of the missing breast and implies a double loss—of the breast and the sensation of the hand that held it.

Far left, Titian, Venus with a Mirror; *left, Pierre-Narcisse Guerin,* Jeune fille en buste; *right, Matuschka and Mark Lyon,* The Hand, *1992*

Ludwig Bemelmans,
Dodo D'Hamburg

● THE CREATOR of Madeleine, Ludwig Bemelmans, steps out of the playroom and into a bar—depicting a woman who's happy to be looked at, and who, even if there isn't a mirror, is looking at herself.

● AS A HAPLESS PROSTITUTE in *The Owl and the Pussycat*, Barbra Streisand parodies the notion that not all girls say hands off—even if those hands are self-applied.

BREAST-SCAPES

"Between her breasts is my home, between her breasts,
Three sides set on my space and fear, but the fourth side is rest.
Sure and a tower of strength, 'twixt the walls of her breasts."
—D. H. Lawrence, "Song of a Man Who Is Loved"

Nestling at the bosom is a very distinct form of bliss, if a repeated one—a sweet satisfaction that is almost a rerun of the hazy film of early memory, recalling the original experience of satiation. When Keats wrote, "Pillowed upon my fair love's ripening breast, / To feel for ever in a sweet unrest," he was referring to this state of perfect repose: lulled and enlivened. In the chaos of adult life, rare moments of psychic reprieve can be found in the bosom of things, for if this is the place where we began, it is also the place to which we long to return.

Previous page, Brigitte Bardot in . . . And God Created Woman, *1956; right,* Beyond the Valley of the Dolls, *1970*

◉ FLUFFED UP and ready to rest (or roll), all breasts become one in this very 1960s male fantasy of the ultimate pillow.

THE GREAT SURROUND

Imagining breasts as a protective wall or a fleshy cocoon against the exigencies of the outside world, we have not only likened them to the world around us but have filled our world with breast-approximations. In spaces that mimic breasts' physical form, we are drawn back, in conscious or unconscious ways, to the origins of our contentment. Seeing breasts where they are not, in landscapes or the ripe offerings of the natural world, we pay tribute to their physical magnetism.

THE GRAND TETONS EN BUSTIER

⬤ TWIN PEAKS   Nature's forms tend to recur. Whether breast as mountain or mountain as breast, elegance of form and monumentality rule. The peaks here belong to Wyoming's Tetons (French for "tits").

"Her breasts, like ivory globes
circled with blue,
A pair of maiden worlds
unconquered."
—William Shakespeare,
"The Rape of Lucrece"

Breasts take pride of place in our dream life, too, in the fertile landscapes of the imagination where pleasure palaces, desert isles and secret worlds all reside. Since comfort is material, then we seek out a cushioning pillow in spaces and places that mimic breasts' physical forms—and a promise of bliss.

Henri Cartier-Bresson,
1973

Frederic Church, Cotopaxi, 1855

> *"The proud mountain, rebellious,*
> *virginal and wicked, is a woman for*
> *the alpinist who wills,*
> *at the peril of his life, to violate her."*
> —Simone de Beauvoir

LANDSCAPE AS BODY

Upon sighting America, Columbus described it as an "Edenic nipple" projecting from the mammary globe of the world, making even the new continent familiar. We like to think of nature as human, the more to comfort ourselves from the terror of the unknown, the *not us*. And when anthropomorphized, nature is most often a woman, making an interesting parallel between the unruly familiarity of the fair sex and the earth itself. Nature may be characterized as an ice queen or an earth mother, a place where the explorer can plant his flag or sow his seed—or discover hidden treasure.

Numerous writers have made this association between breasts and terrain. In H. Rider Haggard's *King Solomon's Mines*, for example, danger and discovery lead to a lost cave chock-full of diamonds located (for narrative charge) atop a mammary mountain. The treasure map instructs: "Climb the snow of Sheba's left breast" till you "come to the nipple of the north side. . . ."

● HIGH RISE   These Afghan shrines are mounted on two hills within looking distance of each other—and from a distance, as in this photograph by Carollee Pelos, we can see the purpose of their divine elevation.

". . . a fresh green breast
of the new world."
—F. Scott Fitzgerald

BODY AS LANDSCAPE

From a distance, female contours can seem like whole continents yet to be discovered, a final frontier. Like scalable Everests, breasts emerge from the body's terrain, beckoning the explorer to terra incognita, a destination from whose bourne no traveler wishes to return. Breasts can offer the thrill of the unknown—or the pleasures of cognition, not least an infant familiarity.

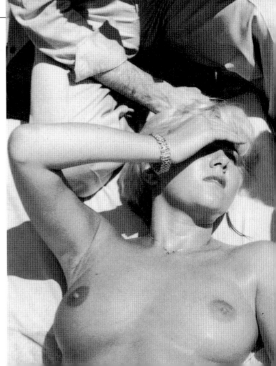

*Plage de la
Croisette, Cannes*

"And the world lay before him . . ."

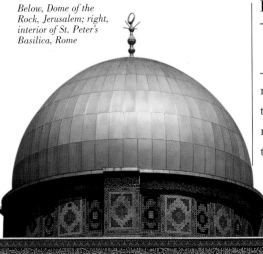

Below, Dome of the Rock, Jerusalem; right, interior of St. Peter's Basilica, Rome

PLEASURE DOMES

uilt in a time when religious buildings were the work of the best architects, breastlike domes represented the crowning achievements of their day. Whether intended or not, domes re-created the familiar bull's-eye, calling the faithful for religious sustenance. First achieved by the Romans in the second century and refined in sixth-century Byzantium (Istanbul), the dome traveled east to Jerusalem before it was further elevated by European

architects for the great cathedrals; it has dominated religious architecture ever since. These grand structures, distinguished by their graceful mounds, towered over all other buildings, creating landscapes that literally bubbled with promise. To enter a domed space is to feel transported; the inverted sphere lifts us closer to the heavens.

Right, Greek Orthodox church, Santorini, Greece; far right, Badshahi Mosque, Lahore, Pakistan

"Her bosom is a marble slab,
whence rise two breasts
like towers on lea. . . ."
—The Arabian Nights

LET THEM DRINK MILK

Among the many tributes built to the breast, the most curious were the pleasure dairies of prerevolutionary France. Designed by leading French artists, these ornamental "temples to milk" were built so aristocratic ladies could spend an idle afternoon milking cows, churning butter and relaxing in a deluxe version of rural simplicity. Marie Antoinette had two pleasure dairies where, dressed in upscale dairy-maid costumes, she accomplished her "chores" with china buckets and Wedgwood pitchers. At the center of these "temples" were white marble cows and images of the multibreasted goddess Isis. The yield of the dairies (built during the nation's food shortage) was mostly iced cheeses and iced creams served in breast-shaped bowls called *jattes tetons*.

JATTES TETONS were rumored to have been modeled on Marie Antoinette's breasts. They were originally designed for the pleasure dairy by Sèvres, who continued to market them until 1885.

THE MILK BAR is the flip side of the pleasure dairy in Stanley Kubrick's fantasy film *A Clockwork Orange*. The breasts here produce milk of a different kind—malevolent, and laced with something stronger than calcium. In this future dystopia, bride-of-Frankenstein bodies mimic their natural functions but with a phallic aggression. There's nothing soft about these breasts (Look out, boys, they may poke your eye out!) as they dispense their juices mechanically to posses of motherless boys.

CITIES OF WOMEN

The fantasy of a civilization, a city or, even better, a planet occupied only by women—a world where breasts are permanently on display—has been around since at least the time of the Amazons. In the nineteenth century, colonial exploits in the East provided a new site in which to locate this fantasy of a "feminatopia," as the harem and the Turkish bath entered the Western imagination. These lush, breast-cluttered places became popular subjects for painters: here was a set piece for male viewing, an "oriental" spectacle stocked with women luxuriating in their own (and each other's) cushioned and cushioning flesh.

While these paintings make the Turkish bath, or *hamman*, look like a highly sexualized zone, in reality they were (and are) places where women socialized, gossiped, learned about grooming and celebrated marriages and births (or mourned deaths) in the exclusive company of other women. And if the *hamman* was painted by men, only women travelers were actually permitted inside. In 1717, English traveler Lady Mary Wortley Montagu kept a diary of her visit to the hot baths at Sophia, where she found some 200 women lounging about. She writes,

"... one little room,
an everywhere."
—John Donne, "The
Good Morrow"

"Women naked in different postures, some in conversation, some working, others drinking Coffee, and many negligently lying on their Cushions while their slaves (girls of 17 or 18) were braiding their hair. . . . There were many among them as exactly proportion'd as ever any Goddess was drawn by the pencil of Guido or Titian."

● EXOTICA   The most celebrated image of the Turkish bath from the Western perspective, Ingres's *The Turkish Bath*, 1862, was born of fantasy: the artist never traveled to Turkey. This luxuriant spectacle leaves us wondering whose hand is fondling the woman's breast on the right—her own or her companion's?

The harem took the Western fantasy of
the Orient to a new extreme, conjuring a
dream of total abandonment in a foreign
world ruled by the laws of indulgence.
Whereas in reality, membership in the
harem was prestigious and coveted (women
received years of education in the fine arts
before being presented to the Sultan), to the
European imagination harems offered a
world of inexhaustible plenitude. To penetrate this hidden world is to discover an
opulent, all-encompassing universe where
breasts, like the sun, rest at its center.

MUGGY WITH EROTIC TORPOR, harem women seem perpetually to await male ravishment (while in fact only eunuchs were allowed entrance). Though harems present an artistically rendered version of the brothel, in the brothel the man is patron, while in the harem the man is king.

● NAKED LOGIC   Before the twentieth century, painting the nude required (for propriety's sake) a logic of context: classical myth, biblical tales, war stories—in short, a raison d'être for nakedness. Nineteenth-century painters, looking for new nude scenarios, hit upon the gloriously imagined spectacle of the Orient to showcase female flesh. Through Western eyes, the harem becomes an exotic peep show.

Gustavo Mancinelli,
The Odalisque

"She is all states, and all princes I,
Nothing else is."
—John Donne, "The Sun Rising"

EROTIC PHOTOGRAPHS, this
one from 1912, emulated the
exotic flavor of the Turkish bath
as portrayed in painting.

THE EASTERN ODALISQUE, or harem concubine, was popularized by early-twentieth-century French painters. Matisse transplanted exotic oriental imagery to the sun-drenched south of France, where his nudes reclined in sultry languor.

Henri Matisse, Odalisque with Raised Arms *(right), 1923, and* Odalisque in Grey Culottes *(far right), 1926*

A TROPICAL EDEN

What some men found in pictures of paradise, others went off to discover in the flesh: a land of women, free from convention—and clothes. While Odysseus tied himself to his ship's mast and plugged his sailors' ears with wax to resist the song of the Sirens, artist Paul Gauguin heeded the call, leaving his wife and five children behind.

OFFERING FRESH FRUIT as a stand-in for her young breast, the Eve of Gaugin's tropical Eden has nothing to do with a fall from grace; she doesn't know of the sinfulness of pleasure.

In the bare-breasted innocence of Tahitian women, Gauguin found the inspiration for his greatest paintings, depicting a paradise where breasts were as plentiful as fruit: "From their coppery breasts trembling melodies arise, and are faintly thrown back from the wrinkled trunks of the coconut-trees. They are the Tahitian songs. . . ."

GAUGUIN'S TAHITIAN MODELS were, he felt, nothing like the Parisian "salon Venuses" who, he said in an 1895 interview, were "indecent, odiously lubricious." Unlike those figures of sexual artifice and ornament, his prelapsarian maidens are pictured as ripening fruits from Mother Earth—not to be conquered by the warrior, but plucked by the gatherer.

"those lovely, golden-nippled breasts . . . so unsuited to corsets."
—Paul Gauguin

GOOD ENOUGH TO EAT

The Eden of plenitude is within our grasp, found in the ordinary offerings of the nearby natural world. The phrase "mother earth" derives from the Latin *terra mater*; in the cosmology of the ancient Greek poet Hesiod, Gaia, the deep-breasted Earth, mates with the male Sky to form the heavens. In other words, we've known since antiquity that female nature is a good provider. In this sweet and available abundance—from the orchard, the meadow, the farm and the garden, to its presence at the table—the temptations

Alphonse Mucha,
Fruit, 1897

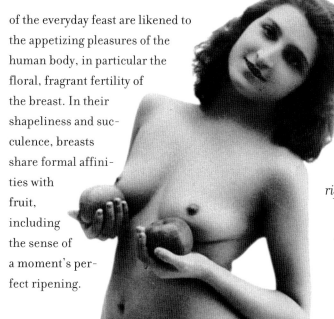

of the everyday feast are likened to the appetizing pleasures of the human body, in particular the floral, fragrant fertility of the breast. In their shapeliness and suc-culence, breasts share formal affini-ties with fruit, including the sense of a moment's per-fect ripening.

"Her small breasts, mounted high, were so round they had less the air of being an integral part of her body than of having ripened there like two fruits."
—*Marcel Proust,*
À la recherche du temps perdu

Kubim 68

FROM PEACHES AND MANGOES to prunes, breasts are commonly likened to nature's sweets. In the cornucopia—fruit overflowing the bowl—the breast is a luscious delight, plump, ripe and waiting to be plucked.

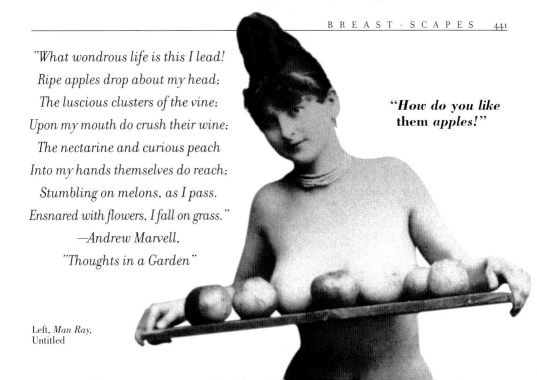

"What wondrous life is this I lead!
Ripe apples drop about my head;
The luscious clusters of the vine;
Upon my mouth do crush their wine;
The nectarine and curious peach
Into my hands themselves do reach;
Stumbling on melons, as I pass.
Ensnared with flowers, I fall on grass."
    —Andrew Marvell,
    "Thoughts in a Garden"

Left, *Man Ray,*
Untitled

"How do you like them *apples!*"

abbondanzas

abundance · angel cakes · antiaircraft guns · apples · areola borealis · B-52s · balboas · balcony · balloons · bananas · bangers · bangles · bassoons · baubles · bazongas · bazonkas · bazoombas · bazooms · bazoongies · beacons · beanbags · beauts · bebops · begonias · bells · berks · Betty Boops · big boppers · big brown eyes · bikini stuffers · billibongs · binoculars · biscuits · blinkers · bobbers · bolt-ons ·

bonbons

bombers · bombshells · bongos · bonkers · boobahs · boobers · boobies · boobs · boondogglers · boopers · boops · bops · bosom · boulders · bouncers · the boys · boy toys · bra buddies · bra stuffers

• breasts • bristols • bronskis • bubbas • bubbies • bubbles • buds • buffers • bulbs • bulges • bullets • bumpers • bumps • buoys • bust • busters • busties • butterbags • butterballs • buttons • caboodles • cams • cannonballs • cans • cantaloups • cartons • carumbas • casabas • cha-chas • challoopahs • charlies • charms • chee-chees •

coconuts

chest • chihuahuas • chimichangas • chiquitas • clackers • cleavage • cleave • columns • cones • congas • corkers • creamers • cream pies • cupcakes • cups • curves • dairies • dingers • dinghies • dirigibles • domes • doodads • doorknobs • doozers • doozies • double wham-mies • dueling banjos • dugs • dumplings • dunes • droopers • dynamic duo • earmuffs • éclairs • eggplants • enchiladas • eyes

· flapjacks · flappers · flesh bulbs · flesh melons · floaters · floats · fog lights · fried eggs · front · gagas · garbos · gazingas · gazongas · the girls · Gel-Paks (implants) · giganzos · gland canyons · glands · globes · globlets · gobdobblers · Gobstoppers · golden bozos · gongas · goombas · grandstand · grapefruits · grillwork · guavas · gumdrops · handles · handsets · hand warmers · hangers · headlights · happy bags · headers · headlamps · headphones · headrests · headsets · hefties · heifers · hemispheres · hills · Hindenburgs · hogans · honeydews · honkers · hood ornaments · hoo-has · hooters · hotcakes · howitzers · hubcaps · huffies · jersey cities · huge tracts of land · humdingers · hush puppies · ICBMS · jawbreakers

· Jell-O molds · jibs · jigglers · jiggly bits · jobbers · joy boys · joy toys · jugs · jukes · jumbos · kalamazoos · kazongas · kazoos · kettledrums · knickknacks · knobbers ·

kanakas

knobs · knockers · kongas · kumquats · lactallickas · lactoids · lemons · life preservers · lip fodder · llamas · loaves · loblol- lies · lollipops · love bubbles · love fruit · love melons · love muffins · lulus · lunch wagon · lungs · macaroons · mambos · mammaries · mammies · mammoth mammary · mams · mangos · maracas · marangos · maraschinos · marimbas · marsh- mallows · mausers · meatballs ·

manchesters

meat loaves · melons · milk bottles · milk cans · milk fountains · milk shakes · Milky Way · Minneapolis/Saint Paul · missiles · molehills ·

mommas · mondos · Montezumas · monuments · moo moos · mosqui-
to bites · mother lode · mounds · mountain peaks · mountains ·
muchachos · muffins · mulligans · mushmellons · nancies · nectarines
· les nénés

mezzanines

· niblets ·
nibs · nin-
nies · nippers · nippies · nipple holders · nippleoons · nippleos · nodes
· nodules · noogies · nose cones · nose warmers · nubbies · num-nums
· nungas · oboes · orbs · ottomans · pair · paperweights · peaches ·
pillows · pimples · pink-nosed puppies · playground · PT boats ·
pumpkins · pylons · rack · raisins · rib cushions · rib rack · rivets ·
les roberts · les roploplos · roundies · sacks ·
sandbags · satellites · saucers · schooners · oompahs

scones · scoops · set · shakers · shebas ·
shelf · shermans · shimmies · silos · smoothies
snuggle pups · spark plugs · specials · spheres · sponge cakes ·
spuds · squirt guns · stacks · stuffing · sugarplums · sweater kittens ·
sweater puffs · sweet rolls · swingers · Tahitis · tamales · tattlers · teacups
· teats · tetons · thangs · thingamajigs · tidbits · titbits ·
ta tas tits · titskis · titters · titties · tomatahs · tomatoes ·
tom-toms · tooters · topside · torpedoes · tortillas · totos · twangers ·
tweakers · tweeters · twin beds · twin peaks · the twins · twofers ·
tympanies · U-boats · udders ·
umlauts · upper deck · veiled twins · yin & yang
wahwahs · waldos · wangdoodles · watermelons · whoppers · wind-
jammers · Winnebagos · wollopies · yabos · yams · ya yas · zeppelins

PHOTO CREDITS

Unless otherwise specified, copyright on the works reproduced lies with the respective photographers, agencies and museums. Despite extensive research, it has not always been possible to establish copyright ownership. Where this is the case, we would appreciate notification.

page ii: Bert Stern; page vi: (left) Tattoo Museum/Henk Schiffmacher; (right) Ursula Markus/Photo Researchers, Inc.; page vii: Paramount (courtesy Kobal); page viii: The Advertising Archives/Photofest; page ix: Francis G. Mayer/CORBIS; page x: © Gianni Dagli Orti/CORBIS; page xii: © Scala/Art Resource, N.Y. (Galleria Borghese, Rome); page xiii: © Douglas Faulkner/Photo Researchers, Inc.; page xiv: © Tim Davis/Photo Researchers, Inc.; page xv: Alan Chasanoff Photographic Collection/Museum of Fine Arts, Houston; page xvii: © SuperStock; page xviii: © SuperStock; page xxi: Bettmann-UPI/CORBIS; page xxiv: © 2001 Artists Rights Society (ARS), N.Y./The Menil Collection, Houston

AN EMBARRASSMENT OF RICHES page 3: © Musée d'Orsay, Paris/Giraudon, Paris/SuperStock; page 5: Alan Grant/TimePictures; page 6: © Vaga/private collection/Art Resource, N.Y.; page 7: Tate Gallery, London/Art Resource, N.Y.; page 8: (left) CORBIS/Danny Lehman; (right) The Akehurst Bureau; page 9: Joyce Tenneson; pages 10–11: Greg Friedler; page 12: © Musée du Louvre, Paris/AKG, Berlin/SuperStock; page 13: © Scala/Art Resource, N.Y.; page 14: © Ernst Hass/Hulton/Archive; page 15: Greg Friedler; page 16: Getty Images; page 17: © Scala/Art Resource, N.Y. (Museo del Prado, Madrid); page 18: Musée d'Orsay/Art Resource, N.Y.; page 19: © M. H. de Young Museum, San Francisco/SuperStock; page 20: © Darlaine Honey/Trevillion Picture Library; page 21: (left) IMP/George Eastman House, Rochester, N.Y.; (right) The Kobal Collection; pages 22, 23: Pierre Bonte; page 24: The Metropolitan Museum of Art, H. O. Havemeyer Collection, Bequest of Mrs. H. O. Havemeyer, 1929 (29.100.62). Photograph, 1986, The Metropolitan Museum of Art; page 25: (left) © Horace Bristol/CORBIS; (right) Naomi Johnson Ziegfeld, George Rinehart/CORBIS; page 26: (left) The Granger Collection, N.Y.; (right) © 2001 Artists Rights Society (ARS), N.Y./Tate Gallery, London. Bequeathed by Frank Stoop, 1933; page 27: (left) Jewel (courtesy Kobal); (middle) *Ada*, 1982, © The Estate of Robert Mapplethorpe. Courtesy Art + Commerce Anthology; (right) © Christie's Images; page 28: © Museo Nazionale Romano, Rome/Canali PhotoBank, Milan/SuperStock; page 29:

Capella Medici, Florence/Bridgeman Art Library International, Ltd.; page 30: © Archivio Iconografico, S.A./CORBIS; page 31: © Museo del Prado, Madrid/AKG/SuperStock; page 32: Kinsey Institute; page 33: Christian Rodin; page 34: Photofest; page 35: (left) © Ali Meyer/Naturhistorisches Museum, Vienna/Bridgeman Art Library International, Ltd.; (right) Photofest; page 36: © Christie's Images; page 37: © Juan Echeverria/Liaison Agency; page 38: © Bruce Gilden/Magnum Photos; page 39: Jean Gaumy/Magnum Photos; page 40: Mary Evans Picture Library; page 41: Photofest; page 42: Manet/private collection/SuperStock; page 43: Bruce Gilden/Magnum Photos

A FEAST FOR THE EYES page 45: John Willis; page 46: Ursula Markus/Photo Researchers, Inc.; page 47: Barnaby Hall/Getty Images; page 48: Shelburne Museum, Shelburne, Vt.; page 49: United Artists (courtesy Kobal); page 50: Barnaby Hall/Getty Images; page 51: Photofest; page 52: Güler Uger; page 53: Photograph by Imogen Cunningham, © 1978 The Imogen Cunningham Trust; page 54: National Museum of Abidjan, Republic of the Ivory Coast/Explorer/ SuperStock; page 55: Wellcome Institute Library, London; page 56: Barnaby Hall/Getty Images; page 58: © Christie's Images; page 59: © AKG Photo, London; page 60: © Biophoto Associates/Photo Researchers, Inc.; page 61: David Gifford/

Science Photo Library/Photo Researchers, Inc.; pages 62–63: © AKG Photo, London; page 64: © Musée du Louvre, Paris/SuperStock; page 65: © Christie's Images; pages 66, 67: © RMN/Art Resource, N.Y. (Musée Municipal, Leon); page 68: Kress Collection, Washington, D.C./ Bridgeman Art Library International, Ltd.; page 69: © RMN/ Art Resource, N.Y. (Châteaux de Versailles et de Trianon, Versailles); page 70: Mary Evans Picture Gallery; page 71: Wellcome Institute Library, London; page 72: © AKG, Berlin/SuperStock; page 75: (left) © Scala/Art Resource, N.Y. (Palazzo Arcivescovile, Siena); (right) The Metropolitan Museum of Art, John Stewart Kennedy Fund, 1910 (10.189). Photograph, 1988, The Metropolitan Museum of Art; page 76: © Hermitage, St. Petersburg/Bridgeman Art Library International, Ltd./Christie's Images; page 77: © Koninklijk Museum voor Schone Kunsten, Antwerp/ Bridgeman Art Library International, Inc.; page 78: © Christie's Images; page 79: Jan Gossaert Eric/Art Resource, N.Y.; page 80: © RMN/Art Resource, N.Y. (Musée d'Orsay, Paris); page 81: Martine Franck/Magnum Photos; page 82: Mary Evans Picture Library; page 83: (left) Chaloner Woods/Liaison Agency; (middle and right): Assistance Publique-Hopitaux de Pari/Musée; page 84: (left) Mary Evans Picture Gallery; (right) Bettmann/ CORBIS; page 87: Mary Ellen Mark

THE SHADOW OF YOUNG GIRLS IN BLOOM page 89: © Christie's Images; page 90: © Harry Gruyaert/Magnum Photos; page 91: © Marc Riboud/Magnum Photos; page 92: © Ferdinando Scianna/Magnum Photos; page 93: © Sally Mann/courtesy Edwynn Houk Gallery, N.Y.; page 95: Paul Bergon/Société Française de Photographie, Paris; page 96: © Galleria degli Uffizi, Florence/SuperStock; page 97: © Nancy Honey/Getty Images; page 98: © Gen Nishino/Liaison Agency; page 99: Getty Images; page 102: CORBIS; page 103: © André Fatras/Liaison Agency; page 104: © 2001 Artists Rights Society (ARS), N.Y./ADAGP, Paris/private collection/Bridgeman Art Library International, Ltd.; page 105: © 2001 The Munch Museum/The Munch-Ellingsen Group/Artists Rights Society (ARS), N.Y./National Gallery, Oslo/AKG, Berlin/SuperStock; page 106: Photodisc; page 107: © 2001 Artists Rights Society (ARS), N.Y./ADAGP, Paris/Pierre Matisse Gallery/SuperStock; page 108: © Serge Nazarieff Collection/The Akehurst Bureau; page 110: Darren Modricker/CORBIS; page 111: Laura Strauss; page 112: Mary Ellen Mark; page 113: Laura Strauss; page 114: © Hulton/Archive; page 115: Photofest; page 117: © 2001 Artists Rights Society (ARS), N.Y./Christie's Images; page 118: The Kobal Collection; pages 119, 120–121, 122, 123: Photofest; page 124: American International (courtesy Kobal); page 125: © Benainous/Scorceletti/Liaison Agency

SHAPING THE SILHOUETTE page 127: © Bettmann-UPI/CORBIS; page 129: Hulton Getty Picture Library; page 130: Walter Weissman/Globe Photos: page 131: Andrea Renault/Globe Photos; pages 132–133: © Liaison Agency; pages 134–135: © David Parker/Science Photo Library/Photo Researchers, Inc.; page 136: (left) © Tate Gallery, London/Art Resource, N.Y.; (middle left) © Erich Lessing/Art Resource, N.Y. (National Gallery, London); (middle right) © Ferdinando Scianna/Magnum Photos; (right) Universal (courtesy Kobal); page 137: Miramax (courtesy Kobal); page 138: © Villa of Casale, Piazza Armerina, Sicily/Silvio Fiore/SuperStock; pages 138–139: © Erich Lessing/Art Resource, N.Y.; page 140: © National Portrait Gallery, London/SuperStock/Photofest; page 141: © The Granger Collection, N.Y.; page 142: Collection Kharbine-Tapabor; page 143: © The Granger Collection, N.Y.; page 144: Bettmann/CORBIS; page 145: © Musée des Augustins, Toulouse, France/Explorer/SuperStock; pages 146–147: CORBIS; page 148: Mary Evans Picture Library; page 149: © Bettmann/CORBIS; page 150: Mary Evans Picture Library; page 152: © Bettmann/CORBIS; page 153: Archives Larousse/Art Resource, N.Y.; page 154: Photofest; page 155: Mary Evans Picture Library; page 156: Varga Girl, Alberto Vargas, © 1943 Hearst Corporation; page 157: Photofest; page 158: courtesy Maidenform, Inc.; page 159: The

Advertising Archives; page 160: Photofest; page 161: John Chillingworth/Picture Post/CORBIS; page 162: The Advertising Archives; page 163: Photofest; page 164: (left) © Nancy Honey/Stone; (right) Photograph by William Mercer McLeod; page 165: © Reuters/CORBIS; page 166: The Advertising Archives; page 167: courtesy Bioform by Charnos; page 168: Matt Mendelson/CORBIS; page 169: Dan Lecca

GETTING THEM RIGHT page 171: Paramount (courtesy Kobal); page 173: Mary Evans Picture Library; page 175: Earl and Nazima Kowall/CORBIS; page 176: Photofest; page 177: The Advertising Archives; page 178: © Barry King/Liaison Agency; page 179: © Barry King/Liaison Agency; page 180: courtesy Triumph; page 182: CORBIS/Stock Market; page 183: © Bettmann-UPI/CORBIS; page 184: (left top) Retna/Cliff Lipson; (left bottom) Retna/Steve Granitz; (left middle top) Lisa Rose/Globe; (left middle bottom) Henry McGee/Globe; (right middle top) Retna/Steve Granitz; (right middle bottom) Retna/Paul Smith; (right top) Retna/Steve Granitz; (right bottom) Retna/Paul Smith; page 185: (left) Alpha, London/Globe; (right) Alec Michael/Globe; page 186: © David Hurn/Magnum Photos; page 187: © Yvonne Hemsey/Liaison Agency; pages 188–189: first published as "Dr. Jack Makes His Rounds," by Pierre Houles, in *Esquire* magazine, Hearst Corporation; pages

190, 192–193: © Bettmann-UPI/CORBIS; pages 194–195: courtesy Dr. George Baraka, N.Y.; pages 196–197: Malcolm Roth, M.D.; page 199: © Bettmann/CORBIS

THE JEWEL IN THE CROWN page 201: Jerome Tisne/Getty Images; page 203: © 2001 Artists Rights Society (ARS), N.Y./ADAGP, Paris/Burstein Collection/CORBIS; page 205: © Musée du Louvre, Paris/SuperStock; page 206: (left) © Graham Ovenden Collection/The Akehurst Bureau; (right) private collection/Burstein Collection/CORBIS; page 207: Stephane Coutelle; page 208: Hulton Getty Picture Library; page 210: © 2001 Artists Rights Society (ARS), N.Y./© Estate of Alice Neel, courtesy Robert Miller Gallery; page 211: © Liaison Agency; page 212: Güler Uger; page 213: © Beth B.; page 214: © SuperStock; page 215: (left) © Christie's Images; (middle) The Advertising Archives; (right) © National Gallery of Ancient Art, Rome/Canali Photo Bank, Milan/SuperStock; page 216: © Archivio Iconografico, S.A./CORBIS; page 217: © Edimédia/CORBIS; page 218: © 2001 Kingdom of Spain, Gala-Salvador Dalí Foundation/Artists Rights Society (ARS), N.Y./private collection/Bridgeman Art Library International, Ltd./SuperStock; page 219: Tate Gallery, London/Art Resource, N.Y.; page 220: Kinsey Institute; page 221: © Uwe Scheid Collection, Überherrn; page 222: Allan Chasanoff Photographic

Collection/Museum of Fine Arts, Houston; page 223: Archiv für Kunst Geschichte, Berlin/AKG, London; page 225: © Daniel Simon/Liaison Agency; page 226: (top) Photofest; (bottom) AP Photos; page 227: Rick Grossman; page 228: Barnaby Hall/Phonica; page 229: Charles Gatewood; pages 230–231: © Kirk Condyles/Impact Visuals

THE VEILED EROTIC page 233: © Worcester Art Museum, Worcester, Mass./SuperStock; page 235: © Galleria degli Uffizi, Florence/SuperStock; page 236: Bibiothèque Nationale de France; page 237: Hulton Getty Picture Library; page 238: © Giraudon/Château de Loches, France/Bridgeman Art Library International, Ltd.; page 239: Barnaby Hall; page 240: © Christie's Images; page 241: © Museo Civico Revoltella, Trieste, Italy/SuperStock; page 242: © Elliott Erwitt/Magnum Photos; page 243: © Giraudon/Art Resource, N.Y. (Musée des Beaux-Arts, Rennes, France) page 244: Mary Evans Picture Library; page 245: © Robert Flynt, 1996 (untitled chromogenic photograph, 20" x 24", courtesy of the artist and the Wessel + O'Connor Gallery, N.Y.); page 246: © Jonathan Blair/CORBIS; page 247: Mary Evans Picture Library; page 248: (left) Kunsthistorisches Museum, Wein, Germany; (right) © Daniel Simon/Liaison Agency; page 249: © Stadelsches Culture Institute, Frankfurt, Germany/AKG, Berlin/SuperStock; page 250: Art Resource, N.Y.; page

251: Tintoretto (1518–1594), *Portrait of a Young Woman Revealing Her Breasts*. Prado, Madrid/Scala Picture Library/Art Resource, N.Y.; page 252: Photofest; page 253: Photofest; pages 254–255: Tattoo Museum/Henk Schiffmacher; page 256: Auguste Bernard (called Bernard d'Agesci, French, 1756–1829), *Lady Reading Letters of Heloise and Abelard*, c. 1780. Mrs. Harold T. Martin Fund; Lacy Armour Endowment; Charles H. and Mary F. S. Worcester Collection, 1994.430, © The Art Institute of Chicago. All rights reserved; page 257: © Francis G. Mayer/CORBIS; page 258: SuperStock; page 259: Man Ray Estate; page 260: courtesy of Fredericks of Hollywood; page 261: Kinsey Institute; page 262: Photofest; page 263: © Trevor Watson/The Akehurst Bureau; page 264: Hulton-Deutsch Collection/CORBIS; page 265: © Henry Diltz/CORBIS; page 266: Kinsey Institute; page 267: Photofest

AMERICAN ICON page 269: Photofest; pages 271, 272: © Bettmann/CORBIS; pages 274–275: The Advertising Archives; page 276: The Advertising Archives; pages 277, 278: © Scott Swanson/Archive Photos; page 279: (left) © Bettmann/CORBIS; (right) © SuperStock/CORBIS; page 280: CORBIS; page 281: SuperStock; page 284: Culver Pictures; page 285–293: Photofest; pages 294–295: The Kobal Collection; pages 296, 297: Photofest; page 298: (left) © Reuters NewsMedia, Inc./CORBIS; (right) © SuperStock;

page 299: CORBIS; pages 300–302: © Bettmann/CORBIS; page 303: AP Photo; page 304: © Cotla/Liaison Agency; page 305: © Hulton/Archive; page 306: Kinsey Institute; page 307: courtesy of Something Weird Video and Shock Films; page 308: Rick Grossman; page 309: (left) Photofest; (right) Rick Grossman; page 310: Photograph by Sylvia Plachy; page 311: Bild Lilli advertisement. Lilli promotional, 1955. Published in *Forever Barbie* by M. G. Lord, Balantine Books

MILITANT EXPOSURE page 315: © Hulton/Archive; page 317: Photofest; page 318–319: The Metropolitan Museum of Art, Rogers Fund, 1907 (07.286.84). Photograph © 1991 The Metropolitan Museum of Art; page 320: courtesy of DC Comics; page 321: (left) © Bettmann/CORBIS; (right) Photofest; pages 322–323: © Ephesus Museum, Turkey/ET Archive, London/SuperStock; page 324: © Palazzo Pitti, Florence/Bridgeman Art Library International, Ltd.; page 325: Institut Amatller D'Art Hispanic; page 327: © Jo Spence Archive, London; page 328: © Matuschka; page 329: Bettmann/CORBIS; page 330: © Wally McNamee/CORBIS; page 331: © Joe Traver/Liaison Agency; pages 332–333: Bettmann-UPI/CORBIS; page 335: © The Granger Collection, N.Y.; page 336: (left) © Musée du Louvre, Paris/SuperStock; page 337: © Erich Lessing/Art Resource, N.Y. (Musée d'Orsay, Paris); page 338: (left) Reuters/Hulton Getty

Picture Library; (right) Photo by Arnaldo Magnani/Liasion Agency; page 339: (left) © David David Gallery, Philadelphia/SuperStock; (right) Gamma; page 340: © Erich Lessing/Art Resource, N.Y.; page 341: © 2001 Estate of Pablo Picasso/Artists Rights Society (ARS), N.Y./Musée de Picasso, Idem/SuperStock

WE'LL SHOW 'EM! page 343: Mary Ellen Mark; page 345: Lisa Yuskavage; page 347: (left) Art Resource, N.Y.; (right): Duane Michals; page 349: (left) © Museo de Santa Cruz, Toledo, Spain/Bridgeman Art Library International, Ltd.; (right) courtesy of Cindy Sherman and Metro Pictures; page 350: © Musée du Louvre, Paris/SuperStock; page 351: © Christine Schlesinger; page 353: Staatliche Museum, Berlin/PreuBischer Kulturbesitz Nationalgalerie/Photo by Jorg P. Anders, Berlin; page 354: Jo Spencer Archive/London/*History of the Breast*, Alfred A. Knopf; page 355: © 2001 Artists Rights Society (ARS), N.Y./ADAGP, Paris/Christie's Images; page 356: © 2001 Artists Rights Society (ARS), N.Y./National Portrait Gallery, Smithsonian Institution/National Museum of Women in the Arts, Washington, D.C./Art Resource, N.Y.; page 357: © 2001 Artists Rights Society (ARS), N.Y./National Portrait Gallery, Smithsonian Institution/Art Resource, N.Y.; © Estate of Alice Neel; page 358: reproduced by special permission of